THE U.S. WAR
drive against
CHINA

What it means for workers

struggle-la-lucha.org

BALTIMORE • LOS ANGELES • NEW YORK

**The U.S. War
drive against
CHINA
What it means for workers**

ISBN: 9798342498661

Struggle for Socialism ★ La Lucha por Socialismo
Struggle-La-Lucha.org
X: @StruggleLaLucha
Facebook.com/strugglelalucha
info@struggle-la-lucha.org

East Coast office
2011 N. Charles St., Baltimore, MD 21218
Phone: 443.221.3775

West Coast office
5278 W. Pico Blvd., Los Angeles, CA 90019
Phone: 323.306.6240

Fonts used are Minion and Encode Sans
Book design: Lallan Schoenstein

CONTENTS

INTRODUCTION

Sharon Black

October 1, 2024, marks the 75th anniversary of China's earth-shaking revolution, which broke the chains of feudal slavery and imperialist domination.

The Communist Party of China, under the leadership of Mao Zedong, commonly known as Chairman Mao, both inside China and among the world's oppressed, did what was considered near impossible. The revolution ended China's "Century of Humiliation," which began with the British imperialists' First Opium War in 1839.

Widespread famine, floods, and forced labor, as well as severely shortened lifespans, marked the era of imperialist domination. China's huge landmass and difficult terrain made it seemingly impossible to unite the diverse population, including its numerous ethnic groups.

In 1949, only 20% of the population could read, and the life expectancy was 35 years. China was primarily a rural peasant economy; its working class was tiny in comparison. There was almost no industrialization or education. But by 1975, the revolution had increased life expectancy to 65.5 years.

The newly founded People's Republic of China, under the banner, "Women hold up half the sky," abolished arranged marriage, child brides, and concubinage. The status of women was uplifted and enshrined in the 1950 Marriage Law and the Land Law.

In the last 75 years, progress for the masses and China's working class has been remarkable.

In 2012, China's President Xi Jinping, General Secretary of the CPC Central Committee, vowed to eradicate the vestiges of extreme poverty by 2020. Despite the additional challenges posed by the COVID-19 pandemic, the Chinese government proudly proclaimed the eradication of extreme poverty on November 23, 2020.

The World Bank, indeed no friend of the Communist Party of China, declared that China has lifted over 850 million people out of poverty. "By any measure, the speed and scale of China's poverty reduction is historically unprecedented. With this, China has contributed close to three-quarters of the global reduction in the number of people living in extreme poverty."

China is now a world scientific power. It has built high-speed trains and affordable electric cars, reduced pollution and carbon emissions, and engaged in space exploration. The People's Republic of China's accomplishments have spanned the gamut from health care to education and sports.

China is the world's second-largest economy by nominal GDP (Gross Domestic Product), behind the United States, and since 2017 has been the world's largest economy when measured by purchasing power parity (PPP).

GDP is the monetary market value of all final goods and services made within a country during a specific period. What is not measured by this standard is how that is distributed.

PPP is an alternative way to measure GDP that takes into account the differences in the cost of living between countries. It adjusts the GDP figures to reflect the actual purchasing power of a country's currency. When measured by PPP, China's economy has been larger than that of the United States since 2017. The cost of living in China is generally lower than in the United States. This means that the same amount of money can buy more goods and services in China than in the U.S.

The development of the Belt and Road Initiative (BRI) by China, in contrast to the International Monetary Fund (IMF), which demands austerity and cutbacks for loans, has contributed to the developing countries of the Global South.

The BRI is aimed at building infrastructure that links land and sea. In Africa, this includes railways in Kenya, an electric railway in Ethiopia, and hydropower stations in Uganda. Washington, which does not contribute to local development, mainly ships weapons and war munitions to Africa, building AFRICOM — the U.S. Africa Command, a unified combat command of the Pentagon.

Global class war and China

Revolutionary change and the struggles of the working class don't happen in isolation; international events and global pressures influence them. The same applies to the material conditions that shape them.

What the Communist Party of China and the Chinese working class have faced, whether through external or internal pressure, trade wars, attempts at dismemberment, military threats, or hot war, can best be described as a global class war. This struggle primarily pits U.S. imperialism against the working class worldwide, especially in countries intent on building socialism and liberating themselves from imperialist control.

The approach of U.S. monopoly capitalism has not, at any moment, adopted a hands-off policy regarding building socialism in China, nor, for that matter, anywhere else in the world. They are for intervention against socialism everywhere.

It's important to underscore that in the decades preceding the success of the 1949 revolution, the United States military and government were already playing a role in attempting to defeat the Chinese communist revolutionaries by supplying arms to the reactionary Kuomintang.

Both the bloody Korean and Vietnam wars were equally about containing, encircling, and strangling China, along with defeating the liberation aspirations of the Korean and Vietnamese people.

The Pentagon visited unfathomable destruction on both northern Korea and Vietnam. It bombed North Korea to rubble and engaged in carpet bombing and deforestation in Vietnam. An estimated 2.5 million Koreans lost their lives, and the estimated deaths of Vietnamese range from 1 to 3 million. The people of both the Democratic People's Republic of Korea and the Socialist Republic of Vietnam successfully moved heaven and earth to rebuild.

The 1989 reactionary Tiananmen Square "student rebellion" characterized as a massacre by the West and later exposed as a lie might possibly be described as a much earlier attempt, failed as it was, at "color revolution" (the name given to Western-backed attempts at regime change starting with the Rose Revolution in the country of Georgia in 2003).

Throw in the Dalai Lama and the CIA-led "Tibetan independence movement," and the Falun Gong project, and you can see the pattern of lies meant to turn all manner of sympathy against the CPC and direct efforts to divide and dismember the People's Republic of China.

The key to China's ability to hold off counter-revolution and to weather imperialist schemes is that the Communist Party of China and its government, backed by the People's Liberation Army, have continued to hold state power in the name of the working class. China continues to have a planned economy based on the state-owned infrastructure.

Today's heightened danger

The present decade has brought bigger challenges. The maneuvers by U.S. imperialism have been increasingly more dangerous and point in the direction of a hot war centered around Taiwan. The U.S. NATO proxy war against Russia and the increasing regional war in Western Asia, with Palestine as its central flash point, should be seen as one.

What undergirds and fuels this crisis is the contraction of monopoly capitalism. More than ever, the U.S. economy relies less on production for use and more on spending and development for what is popularly called the military-industrial complex. The capitalist banking system is intertwined with these developments. It is the super fuel for inflation and the deepening impoverishment of the broader working class, making larger war inevitable.

Lenin's thesis on imperialism is more important than ever. The drive toward war is independent of political administrations or individual intentions, regardless of how venal or corrupt. As the global capitalist crisis deepens, the U.S. imperialist system is propelled toward wider war.

Our role in the "belly of the beast" is clear. The global working class, including U.S. workers, who increasingly embody a diverse collective of nations, must be united in solidarity with the working class of China.

The vast majority of the people of the United States have nothing in common with the multi-trillion dollar bankers and war profiteers who are promoting the war buildup against China.

This book, "**The U.S. War Drive Against China: What it means for workers,**" is an effort to expose the increasing danger of a U.S. war against China and to reveal the real enemies of the working class.

What it means for workers

Poor People's Campaign march in 1968.

Sharon Black | May 27, 2022

Poor People's Campaign and China's anti-poverty program

On May 12, 1968, Dr. Martin Luther King Jr.'s Poor People's Campaign officially began with a Mother's Day march led by Coretta Scott King and welfare mothers.

I was barely 18 years old. Pregnant with my son and filled with the kind of hope that only the young possess — who know little of the hardships ahead — I participated in the Poor People's Campaign.

My neighbors were from Appalachia; my mother from the coal mining area of eastern Pennsylvania. As much as I was motivated by empathy for the people I loved who were my family and neighbors, it was the civil rights movement that lit a fire inside of me.

So when I saw a flier posted by a group of Vista workers soliciting people to go with them to the D.C. Poor People's Campaign, I called immediately.

I lied to my parents and pretended to stay with a friend, then left for Washington with a small group of older, certainly more sophisticated, participants. Most of them were graduates from the University of Delaware.

I was the youngest, the only woman at the time. I was awkward; I couldn't accompany them to bars because of my age, had no money and had never eaten in a restaurant.

It wasn't surprising that my new companions found me a burden and deserted me once we arrived in Washington. I never saw them again until we made the trip back to Wilmington, Delaware.

Instead, it was older Black participants, mostly from the South, who took me under their wing. I was taught how to piece together boards, hammer nails and build Resurrection City.

Much of the mud, rain and even the speeches remain a blur. The only thing that stood out was the kindness and care of those Black residents of Resurrection City who took a rather young white kid under their guidance and shelter.

The aims of the Poor People's Campaign were never realized. But that is another story.

U.S. poverty today

The United States has the largest economy in the world, yet it is slipping in every indice of quality of life. At last count, 37.2 million people were living in poverty, an increase of 3.3 million from 2020.

Life span in the U.S. has declined for the first time by over two years. The U.S. has slipped from the 43rd place in the world to 64th in life expectancy.

Class divisions and racism have widened. In essence, "The rich have gotten richer and the poor poorer."

Aid to Dependent Children, founded in 1935 through the Social Security Act, which later became Aid to Families with Dependent Children, the country's main welfare program, was ended in 1997 by the Bill Clinton administration. Notwithstanding the program's history of racism, this was a terrible blow.

It's important to recount this history because mothers, particularly Black mothers from the Welfare Rights Organization, played a leading role in the Poor People's Campaign and in fighting for poor people's rights.

In January 2001, George W. Bush created the White House Office of Faith-Based and Community Initiatives through a series of executive orders. These orders shifted federal funds to religious organizations to deliver formerly government-mandated social services.

This move also had a secondary impact of taking the teeth out of church- and religious-led protests, since religious institutions were now competing for government funds.

What was taking place, going back to the Reagan administration, was a trend popularly referred to as "neoliberalism." It included gutting government spending on social programs, eliminating price controls, deregulating and privatizing services in favor of "free market" capitalism.

The nonprofit sector has grown ever larger, but it has served more to enrich its executive directors and top leaders than to serve the poor. It has attracted young workers who are looking for what they consider "meaningful work," only to encounter poor compensation, resistance to union drives and high burnout rates.

This trend toward private charities and nonprofits was meant to replace the government's responsibility to serve people. The vast amount of wealth produced in this country continued to shift to the war machine, the forces of repression and to fill the pockets of bankers and billionaires.

All of this contrasts with the Communist Party of China (CPC) and the Chinese government, which made eradicating poverty one of its major goals.

A formerly poverty-stricken village in China's Liangshan Yi Autonomous Prefecture was completely rebuilt in three years.

Photo: CGTV

China's anti-poverty program

In 1949, the newly-formed People's Republic of China was faced with momentous tasks. The majority of the population were desperately poor peasants plagued with famine and death. There was almost no industrialization or education.

Edgar Snow documents many of the incredible obstacles that faced the CPC in his book, "Red Star Over China." He gives a firsthand account, and puts human faces to the staggering statistics and suffering of both the peasants and the Red Army.

The commitment to wiping out poverty has its roots in the early period of the People's Republic of China and remains important.

Decades later, in 2012, China's President Xi Jinping, general secretary of the CPC Central Committee, vowed to eradicate the vestiges of extreme poverty by 2020.

Despite the incredible challenges posed by the COVID-19 pandemic, the Chinese government proudly proclaimed the achievement of this herculean effort on November 23, 2020.

The World Bank stated that China has lifted over 850 million people out of poverty. "With this, China has contributed close to three-quarters of the global reduction in the number of people living in extreme poverty."

When humanity looks back, this will be one of the biggest stories of this century.

How did China do it?

It would take a much longer article to explain in full. Of course, one factor is China's economic growth. But that's just a part of the equation. Without a conscious effort by the Chinese government, economic growth in of itself would not have solved the problem.

This government effort was remarkably systematic from top to bottom, from the central government to rural villages to individual families. Every poor family is tracked and assessed individually. Villagers voted to determine who among them should be declared in poverty and when poverty was alleviated.

There were five components: industry, relocation, ecological compensation, education and social security. Social security includes both pensions and Dibao, China's minimum living standard guarantee.

Massive apartment buildings were constructed to relocate people in villages where soil erosion or other conditions made it impossible to sustain a higher standard of life. Contrast this with the continual destruction of public housing and Section 8 programs in the U.S. In addition to deep housing subsidies, China's poor families are guaranteed furniture and televisions.

Emphasis is put on providing stipends and funds for education.

Young urban students and workers, many of them professionals, moved from their relatively comfortable lives to rural villages to participate in this campaign. It reminded me of Cuba's literacy campaign that uplifted young women teachers and tasked them with going into the countryside and the mountains to teach peasants to read and write, making Cuba one of the first Caribbean nations to eradicate illiteracy.

Going in opposite directions

The capitalist West, particularly the U.S., remains cynical and dismisses all that China has accomplished. The media distorts and quibbles about statistics. But this is only possible if you have never experienced how poverty crushes human potential.

What cannot be argued is that socialist China is going in the opposite direction of the capitalist West. Under the leadership of the Communist Party of China, the government is taking on the responsibility of uplifting the population.

In contrast, the U.S. government has shed itself of responsibility for the welfare of the people. Instead, its only duty is to the imperialist banks and billionaires and increasing the repressive apparatus from police to prisons to Pentagon.

Our challenge is to learn from what China has done.

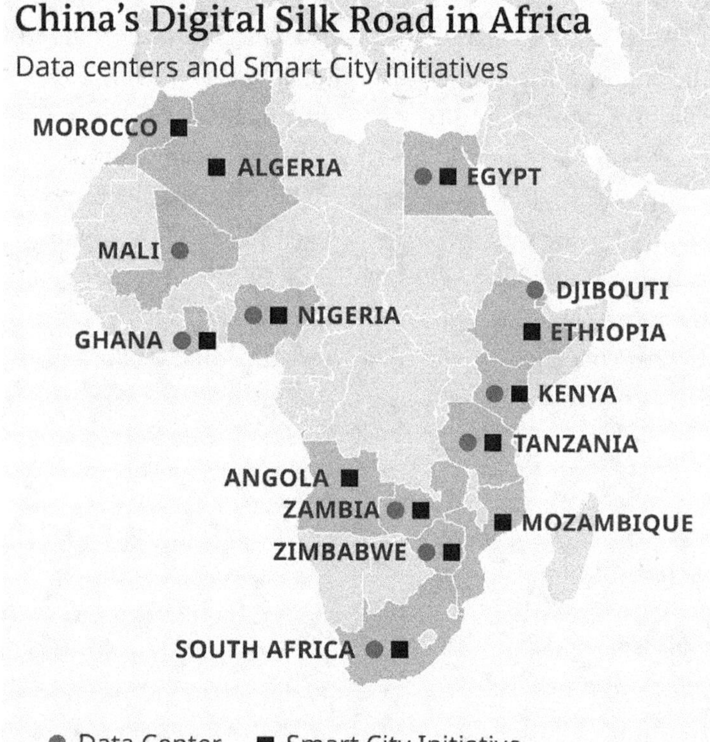

China's Digital Silk Road in Africa
Data centers and Smart City initiatives
MOROCCO
ALGERIA
EGYPT
MALI
DJIBOUTI
NIGERIA
ETHIOPIA
GHANA
KENYA
TANZANIA
ANGOLA
ZAMBIA
MOZAMBIQUE
ZIMBABWE
SOUTH AFRICA
Data Center
Smart City Initiative

John Parker | Sept. 24, 2024

China & Africa: Mutual assistance to defeat imperialism

"Over the past 65 years, China and Africa have forged unbreakable fraternity in our struggle against imperialism and colonialism, and embarked on a distinct path of cooperation in our journey toward development and revitalization. Together, we have written a splendid chapter of mutual assistance."

– **Xi Jinping,** General Secretary of the Central Committee of the Communist Party of China, President of the People's Republic of China

That message was delivered at the Eighth Ministerial Conference of the Forum on China-Africa Cooperation (FOCAC). These powerful words against colonialism and imperialism were said in 2021, during a time when the COVID-19 pandemic especially affected Africa — a continent victim that has endured colonialism and imperialism, as well as the struggle for access to vaccine production.

While the U.S. and Europe put profits before the needs of the victims of colonialism and imperialism, President Xi chose to put those words of solidarity into action.

In that address, President Xi pledged 1 billion vaccine doses to African countries, planning to achieve a 60% vaccination rate in Africa by 2022. In 2021, the cumulative total population coverage with ≥1 dose ranged by country from 0.3%. Xi announced that 600 million doses were donated and 400 million would be produced by joint production projects with Chinese companies and African countries – allowing a further boost in infrastructure and self-determination on the African continent.

The 2024 FOCAC Summit that ended Sept. 6 remained consistent in direction: "Following the Eighth FOCAC Ministerial Conference in Dakar in 2021, we have worked together to fully implement the nine programs and deliver on other outcomes of the meeting."

The relationship is also mutual in benefit. Xi thanked the African countries that helped restore China's lawful seat in the United Nations — last year marked the 50th anniversary of that achievement. China also benefits from Africa's markets and the need for access to the continent's lithium, cobalt, and other minerals.

Turn 180 degrees from this relationship of mutual benefit, and you land at the feet of the International Monetary Fund (IMF) and the World Bank, the imperialist financial institutions demanding austerity cutbacks for loans.

Nigeria is facing the worst economic crisis, with inflation levels not seen in almost three decades due to the austerity demands to secure IMF financing. The Food and Agriculture Organization (FAO) estimates that 26.5 million of Nigeria's 220 million people are food insecure.

The primary architects of the IMF at the Bretton Woods Conference in 1944 — the United States and Britain — ensured that African, Latin American, and Asian self-determination would be denied.

At the end of World War II, the Bretton Woods system established U.S. dominance of the world economy, with the U.S. dollar becoming the world's primary reserve currency for international trade and finance. Most world trade is conducted in U.S. dollars, not local currencies.

The IMF does not contribute to the development of essential infrastructure within a country; instead, it focuses on privatization and significantly reducing social spending.

Zambia faced strong-arm pressure from Canada, the IMF, the World Bank, and First Quantum Minerals in the 1980s. The denial of crucial economic aid jeopardized Zambia's survival. Consequently, the country was forced to privatize its nationalized copper mines in 1990, allowing companies like First Quantum to acquire them cheaply. Additionally, Zambia was forced to appoint a former vice president of the Bank of Canada as the governor of the Bank of Zambia. This guaranteed long-term poverty for Zambian workers … until now.

A turn around pointing upward

"China is ready to use its experience and help Zambia unlock its development potential," said Chinese Ambassador to Zambia Han Jing at a press briefing held Sept. 12 in the Zambian capital of Lusaka after the end of the 2024 FOCAC Summit in Beijing.

Han said China was working with Zambia to make strategic plans for multiple means of power generation, storage, and distribution to help end the current power cuts and make Zambia an electricity exporter.

In 2013, China introduced the Belt and Road Initiative (BRI), aimed at building infrastructure that links land and sea for the economic and social development of the Global South. In Africa, this includes railways in Kenya, an electric railway in Ethiopia, and hydropower stations in Uganda.

While the Belt and Road Initiative focuses on substantial infrastructure development through land and sea projects, the Digital Silk Road is about enhancing digital connectivity and fostering economic growth in a digital landscape for the countries involved.

In 2022, the technology sector in BRI countries saw a remarkable surge in engagement, achieving a staggering 7536% growth compared to the previous year, according to the Africa-China Center for Policy and Advisory.

Many African nations resisted U.S. pressure from the Trump administration against engaging with China, the Africa Policy Research Institute reported. As of September 2021, approximately 70% of the 4G base stations in Africa were built by the Chinese company Huawei. This is alongside the contributions of other Chinese firms in the development of fiber optics throughout the continent.

Which explains why Huawei was targeted by the U.S. Huawei Chief Financial Officer Meng Wanzhou was arrested on Dec. 1, 2018, at Vancouver International Airport by Canadian authorities. She was on a stopover from Hong Kong during a business trip to Mexico City. Meng faced allegations of violating U.S. sanctions that barred trade with Iran and was taken into custody, pending extradition to the United States.

It is not solely the Republicans or Trump who assume a godlike role in their decision-making. In 1998, President

Clinton authorized a missile strike on the Al-Shifa Pharmaceutical Plant in Sudan, resulting in one fatality and injuring others. This action was based on false claims that the facility was manufacturing a VX nerve agent. The plant was crucial for producing essential malaria medication for the African continent. Although Clinton later admitted that the information was incorrect, the U.S. government refused to pay for the devastation caused and did not mind the rising malaria-related fatalities that followed.

At the 2024 Summit of the Forum on China-Africa Cooperation held in Beijing, China outlined its plans to address malaria. According to the World Malaria Report 2023, Africa accounted for 94% of global malaria cases and 95% percent of malaria-related deaths in 2022.

Chinese scientists have developed solutions that resulted in a significant decrease in malaria cases and infection rates in the pilot regions following treatment. The World Health Organization is now collaborating with the CDC's parasitic disease team to expand malaria projects in Tanzania, Zambia, and Senegal.

The Clinton bombing, which contributed to the spread of malaria in Africa, was answered by China's action. It is important to note that during the 1960s, both the Soviet Union and China facilitated the liberation of 17 African nations from colonial rule by providing military support. In fact, the liberation fighters in former Rhodesia received military assistance from China, and one of the earliest freedom fighters to receive training there is the current President of Zimbabwe, Emmerson Mnangagwa. Furthermore, Zimbabwe continues to receive military aid from China.

Threatening the world with rhetoric about remaining "lethal," as Presidential candidate Kamala Harris stated at the DNC, underscores that it ultimately does not matter whether such threats originate from Republicans or Democrats when they enable racism and genocide. African people, like the Palestinian people, know how to fight back; they are not alone in their struggle for liberation.

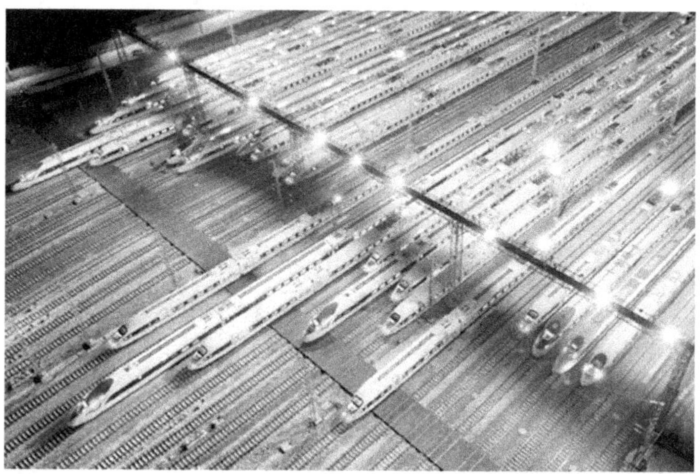

Aerial view of China Railway High-speed bullet trains in Nanjing, Jiangsu Province, January 21, 2019.
Photo: Xinhua

Stephen Millies | Sept. 24, 2024

A retired railroader looks at China's fantastic railroad system

A telling comparison between capitalist decay in the United States and surging economic growth in the socialist People's Republic of China is in their railroad systems.

Between 1950 and 2000, more than 79,000 miles of railroad lines were abandoned in the United States. Passenger service, now run by Amtrak, has withered.

Meanwhile, China has greatly increased its railroad network and now has 100,000 miles of track. China has built twice as many miles of high-speed rail than the rest of the world combined.

Last year, Chinese railways carried 3.68 billion passengers. That's 10 million passengers daily, a hundred times Amtrak's ridership.

China's railroads are on schedule to move 4 billion metric tons of freight in 2024. That's about three times the U.S. total.

Socialist China will invest almost $108 billion in its railroads this year. That's four-and-half times the $23 billion railroad monopolies in the capitalist United States spend on average.

How about urban transport? China has 55 cities with subway systems. Just in Beijing, three new metro lines will open this year.

In contrast, New York City has been trying to complete the construction of the Second Avenue subway for a century. Wall Street's hometown may be the only metropolis with less rapid transit than it had in the 1930s. That's because elevated lines were torn down without replacing them with subways.

The biggest victims of capitalist railroad shrinkage in the U.S. are railroad workers. There were two million workers on the railroads in 1920.

The Great Depression helped reduce railroad employment to 1.5 million workers in 1947. Since then, railroad jobs have fallen by 90%, with just 151,200 railroaders working in August 2024.

That's a smaller number of railroad workers than in 1870, one year after the first transcontinental railroad in the United States was completed. These massive job cuts devastated railroad towns coast to coast.

Railroads and racism

Before any railroads were built in China, 15,000 Chinese immigrants were indispensable to building the transcontinental railroad across the Sierra Nevada mountains in California and Nevada. At least a thousand were killed.

Chinese workers, who were 90% of the Central Pacific's workforce, were paid as low as $26 a month, considerably less than their white counterparts. When they went on strike in 1867 over these dangerous conditions and low pay, their demands were ignored by the wealthy railroad moguls.

These tycoons included Leland Stanford, who founded Stanford University, and Charles Crocker, whose Crocker National Bank was merged into Wells Fargo in 1986.

When you hear reactionaries from Stanford University and its Hoover Institution attack the People's Republic of China, remember that Stanford's endowment includes the blood of Chinese immigrants.

Chinese workers were not given any thanks for their vital contribution. At the May 10, 1969, centennial of the Golden Spike ceremony, marking the transcontinental railroad's completion — now all part of the Union Pacific — Transportation Secretary John Volpe refused even to mention the Chinese railroad workers.

Two years after the Golden Spike, working people in Paris "stormed heaven," in Karl Marx's words, and formed the Paris Commune, the first working-class government. The same year, in Los Angeles, then a village with a population of 6,000, 18 Chinese people were lynched in an 1871 pogrom.

Ten percent of the local Chinese population were murdered. Sixty years later, the city's Chinese community was forced to move so Union Station could be built.

In the capitalist United States, railroads and racism went hand-in-hand. Before the Civil War, 9,000 miles of railroads were built by enslaved Africans.

Thousands more miles of tracks were laid after the Civil War by Black prisoners. Among them was the "steel-driving man" John Henry, who was worked to death building the Chesapeake and Ohio, now part of the CSX system. The capitalist running the C&O was Collis P. Huntington, one of the Central Pacific's founders.

Another big railroad capitalist was the former slave owner Johns Hopkins, whose fortune came from the Baltimore and Ohio Railroad (B&O), now also part of CSX. His loot established Johns Hopkins University and its medical school in Baltimore.

General George Custer had it coming. He died for the Northern Pacific — now part of billionaire Warren Buffett's BNSF — that was invading Lakota Sioux land.

Capitalism vs. socialism

About 41 high-speed trains travel daily between the Chinese capital of Beijing and Shanghai. They take around four-and-a-half hours to make the 819-mile trip.

Amtrak has one train, the Capitol Limited, between Washington D.C. and Chicago. It takes 17.5 hours to cover the 764-mile distance.

None of this is the fault of Amtrak workers. It's the result of decades of a capitalist class allowing much of the railroad system to decay.

On Oct. 1, 1949, Mao Zedong declared that "China has stood up." The People's Republic of China was born. At the time there were maybe 12,000 miles of operable railroad track in the country.

Seventy-five years later, China's railroad network has increased eight times in length and many more times in capacity. Almost all of it is owned and operated by the socialist government. There are 2.2 million railroad workers in China.

U.S. railroads were so dangerous that one in nine rail workers was injured in 1909. One in 205 were killed.

The response of the old Interstate Commerce Commission – abolished in 1996 in the name of deregulation – was to stop collecting these embarrassing statistics. ("The Economic History of the United States" by Ernest Bogart)

Two years ago, railroad tycoons like Warren Buffett refused to agree to sick days for railroaders whose work schedules could include any time of day or night, any day of the week.

We need what the People's Republic of China has: a socialist railroad system. The people need to take over the railroads.

The writer is a retired Amtrak worker and a member of the American Train Dispatchers Association and Transportation Communications International Union.

Wuhan University

Photo: Howchou, CC BY-SA 3.0

Apryle Everly | Sept. 24, 2024

A student's pursuit of justice leads to China

Why China? That's a question I have had to answer a lot these past few months. Whether it be family, friends, or previous co-workers, everyone wants to know why I have chosen to apply to Wuhan University for law school.

I'm 23 years old and a recent graduate of college. I am also the first person in my Black working-class family to graduate from college. Since I was a teenager, I've always wanted to be a lawyer, with my specific interest being international law.

It was my dream to serve as counsel on the International Criminal Court. However, given the recent failure of ICC lawyers to bring Israel and its genocidal supporters to heel, I no longer live under any delusions about international law's capabilities in the current world order.

While it is true that there are a myriad of U.S.-based law schools that provide international law programs for students to enroll in, the problem that I have continuously found myself in is cost. I have no help to finance furthering my education and already have around $20,000 of student loan debt.

The slight humor to this situation is that I'm considered lucky compared to other recent Gen-Z graduates, as the average student loan debt is currently over $37,000. I offer this to give perspective on why I would consider what most have politely told me is a drastic change of scenery.

While I must admit the prospect of such change at first was scary, especially since this would be the furthest I have ever traveled, I now embrace the change. The first two reasons I offer to those who ask are cost and cultural experience. Like so many others my age, I want to receive an education for my passions and have ambitions of turning those passions into a career.

The better option is obvious

The School of International Law at Wuhan University has one of the world's top international law programs and thousands of students worldwide enroll every semester. The total cost for the duration of the program, 2 years, is currently a little over $9,000. In comparison, the tuition costs for Georgetown University Law Center's three-year program are over $79,000 per year. To any student, the better option is obvious.

Most, if not all, young adults in Gen-Z cannot afford to take out loans to cover this amount of money, nor can they attach all their hopes to receiving scholarships from philanthropists who are only interested in receiving a tax write-off.

China has a rich history that more people should want to experience, not to mention their public transportation systems allow both the Chinese people and visitors to fully enjoy what the country has to offer.

It surprised me when I found out that the Chinese government allots money in the form of scholarships to students from dozens of countries around the world, the U.S.

being one of them. All that is required is that an interested student applies directly with the Chinese government,
most likely through an embassy in their country or the university itself.

Unsurprisingly, the U.S., Britain, and Australia are
amongst the lowest student populations to utilize the
scholarship monies provided. This needs to change, as
there should be as few barriers to higher education as possible, despite the ruling class's desire to keep people stuck in
perpetual debt. If the international community welcomes
me with open arms, I think it only makes sense to accept
the invitation and learn from people worldwide.

While I'm sure many may not understand my decision
to go outside the box of U.S. conventionalism, all I have
to offer is that those with my circumstances, will and do
understand. Some have even offered to visit me while I'm
there. I am the first in my family to graduate from college,
and while that is something to celebrate, my story does not
end there. I have always wanted to be part of the international community, to see for myself what is true and what is
not, and to work with others around the world to bring true
justice to the working class.

True international solidarity rooted in the working class
is not something any U.S. law program could ever offer, and
thus, it's not for me anymore. Although I wrote this to explain why I decided to make this decision, I'm hoping that
this gives information to other young people interested in
doing the same.

Biden has slapped a 100% tariff on Chinese electric vehicles.

Chris Fry | June 23, 2024

PART 1

Biden's tariffs on China:
A union worker's response

When Biden was running for office in 2020, he said that Trump's tariffs on Chinese products increased inflation on the public and promised to reduce or eliminate them.

He did not.

Instead, on May 4, the Biden Administration announced a massive tariff increase on imported goods from the People's Republic of China (PRC):

Battery parts (non-lithium-ion batteries)	Increase rate to 25% in 2024
Electric vehicles	Increase rate to 100% in 2024
Facemasks	Increase rate to 25% in 2024
Lithium-ion electrical vehicle batteries	Increase rate to 25% in 2024
Lithium-ion non-electrical vehicle batteries	Increase rate to 25% in 2026
Medical gloves	Increase rate to 25% in 2026
Natural graphite	Increase rate to 25% in 2026
Other critical minerals	Increase rate to 25% in 2024
Permanent magnets	Increase rate to 25% in 2026
Semiconductors	Increase rate to 50% in 2025
Ship to shore cranes	Increase rate to 25% in 2024
Solar cells (whether or not assembled into modules)	Increase rate to 50% in 2024
Steel and aluminum products	Increase rate to 25% in 2024
Syringes and needles	Increase rate to 50% in 2024

Tariffs on medical supplies must be considered particularly bizarre, as the population is still subject to outbreaks of the deadly Covid virus. And public health officials are increasingly alarmed by a new outbreak from the avian H5N1 flu virus which has infected dairy cows and their milk across the country. Many farmworkers who milk cows have become ill from this virus.

A June 3 Scientific American article reports:

The U.S. Centers for Disease Control and Prevention currently recommends that workers on farms where H5N1 has been detected have access to personal protective equipment, or PPE, such as N95 respirators, face masks, goggles and face shields. But it's only a recommendation, Emory School of Medicine Associate Professor Seema Lakdawala says.

In order to prevent bird flu from causing more infections in humans, Lakdawala thinks dairy workers on all farms should have access to and use proper PPE — especially face shields to protect their eyes. Getting workers to wear N95 masks while working all day in hot barns is unlikely, but a face shield would provide at least some protection.

But in terms of the economic effects on workers and the oppressed communities, the most dramatic was the tariff increase was on electric vehicles (EVs), going from Trump's 25 percent to a whopping 100 percent, doubling the price of the cars, placing them out of reach for most of our class.

And Biden tripled tariffs on Chinese-manufactured lithium batteries, going from Trump's 8% to 25%.

The big winner from Biden's tariffs: Global warming

A May 28th article from the Foreign Policy website describes these new tariffs from an environmental perspective:

The winner of the escalating, zero-sum green technology trade war between the United States and China may well be climate change. In the latest surge of election-year techno-nationalism, to protect and advance his green transition and to out-Trump former U.S. President Donald Trump —

President Joe Biden last week imposed a wave of new tariffs on Chinese-made electric vehicles (EVs), batteries, and solar cells as well as other Chinese goods, in addition to retaining all of Trump's tariffs on China.

Scientists are already predicting that 2024 will surpass 2023 as the warmest year globally:

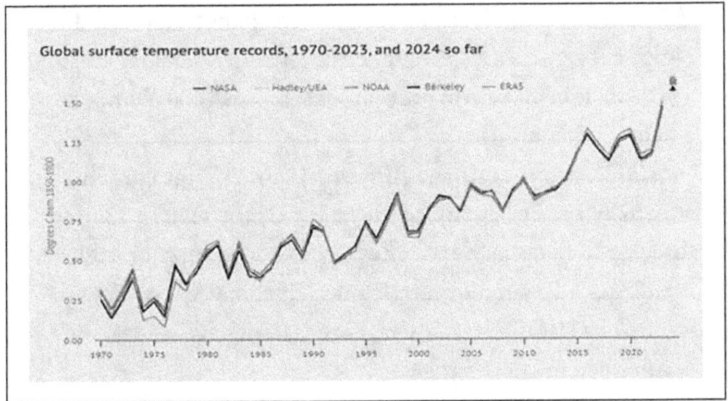

A May 7 CNN article describes some of the catastrophic effects of this on people around the world:

The impacts have been stark. Swaths of Asia have been grappling with deadly heat: schools were closed for millions of children in Bangladesh, rice fields have shriveled in Vietnam, and people in India battled 110 degree Fahrenheit temperatures to vote in recent elections.

Global ocean heat in April was also record-breaking for the 13th consecutive month. Ocean surface temperatures reached 21.04 degrees, the highest on record for any April, and just a fraction below the overall record set in March, according to Copernicus data.

The impact on marine systems is devastating. A mass coral bleaching event occurred this spring, which scientists said at the time could be the worst on record.

As for the U.S., the National Oceanic and Atmospheric Administration (NOAA) has presented a grim hurricane forecast for 2024:

NOAA National Weather Service forecasters at the Climate Prediction Center predict above-normal hurricane activity in the Atlantic basin this year. NOAA's outlook for the 2024 Atlantic hurricane season, which spans from June 1 to Nov. 30, predicts an 85% chance of an above-normal season, a 10% chance of a near-normal season and a 5% chance of a below-normal season.

NOAA is forecasting a range of 17 to 25 total named storms (winds of 39 mph or higher). Of those, 8 to 13 are forecast to become hurricanes (winds of 74 mph or higher), including 4 to 7 major hurricanes (category 3, 4 or 5; with winds of 111 mph or higher). Forecasters have a 70% confidence in these ranges.

In 2021, to pass his corporate-friendly Inflation Reduction Act (IRA), Biden promised a 50 percent to 52 percent reduction in greenhouse gas emissions (compared to 2005 levels) by 2030, zero net emissions by 2050, and 50 percent of all new vehicles being zero-emission by 2030.

But in his campaign to "out-Trump" Trump and protect corporate profit margins and the oil and gas industry, these new tariffs mean that Biden's climate promises go right out the window.

As part of Biden's IRA, billions were allocated for public EV charging stations across the country. Yet by February 2024, there are only 61,000 public chargers in the U.S.

In China, by the end of 2023, there were 2.7 million such chargers, with a 40 percent increase expected this year.

Chris Fry | June 23, 2024

International solidarity, not corporate protectionism, key to union drives, jobs, and higher wages and benefits

On May 16, Biden's White House issued a statement quoting union leaders from the AFL-CIO, the United Steelworkers, the Teamsters, the International Brotherhood of Electrical Workers, and the United Auto Workers all applauding Biden's anti-China tariffs. Most of those union leaders echoed the business leaders who were also on the White House statement, commending Biden for "defending American industries" from Chinese "overcapacity" in production of electric vehicles (ERVs) and their batteries.

Even the supposed environmental group Sierra Club was quoted as supporting Biden's tariffs, despite gasoline-powered vehicles currently producing some 25% of carbon emissions that are accelerating global warming.

But the UAW, under the leadership of Shawn Fain, struck a markedly different tone in its statement supporting the tariffs. There was no defense of American industry. Instead, it condemns "corporate greed" that is "pitting worker against worker, pushing wages lower and lower":

"The UAW applauds today's decisive action from the White House on ensuring that the transition to electric vehicles is a just transition. We have warned for many months that, left to the forces of corporate greed, the EV future was threatened by a race to the bottom, from China to Mexico to right here in the United States. Making sure that major corporations have to pay a price for pitting worker against worker, pushing wages lower and lower, is a key part of a pro-worker trade policy. America's autoworkers, our families, and working-class communities across this country want a trade policy that puts workers first. Today's announcement is a major step in the right direction."

UAW reaches a contract agreement for battery workers.

The historic UAW "Stand Up" 2023 contract, won after a militant strike of all three of the "Big 3" companies (General Motors, Ford and Stellantis), placed their electric vehicle and battery factories under the national contract. This also applies to all jointly owned facilities with other companies, typically with foreign ones.

On June 10, the union reached a tentative agreement covering 1600 workers at the Ultium Cells plant in Lordstown, Ohio, a joint venture between General Motors and a South Korean partner, LG Energy Solution. It produces batteries for G.M. electric vehicles.

The New York Times reports that:

> The Ultium Cells contract calls for moving workers to
> a new wage of $30.50 an hour. Over three years, wages will
> rise to $35 an hour. The national contract signed last fall
> had increased the Ultium Cells starting wage to $26.91,
> up from $16.50 an hour when the plant opened.

China has developed sodium ion batteries to replace lithium ions which are more expensive and much less available.

The Ultium Cells contract also calls for the plant to employ four U.A.W. members as full-time safety representatives, and one full-time industrial hygienist. The union and Ultium workers have raised concerns about working with high-voltage electricity and potentially harmful compounds used in the production of E.V. battery packs.

Some 200 former Lordstown workers who transferred to other plants when GM shuttered the giant plant will soon be transferring to the Ultium plant so they can return to the area.

UAW President Fain indicates that this agreement if ratified by the members, will be a model for negotiations at the other EV and battery plants.

This agreement comes some two months after a historic union organizing drive at the Chattanooga, Tennessee, Volkswagen plant, the first such success in a Southern plant in decades.

The corporate empire strikes back

On June 11,the day after the Ultium agreement, a court-appointed monitor, Neil Barofsky, appointed in a 2020 agreement to prevent the UAW from being taken over by the federal government after a huge corruption scandal, blamed Fain for "retaliation against another union officer". The document "paints a portrait of an organization deeply skeptical of federal efforts to keep the union free from corruption — in stark contrast to Fain's public image as an ethics-centered activist."

No actual charges of corruption are made by Barofsky, and Fain strongly denies any wrongdoing:

> "Taking our union in a new direction means sometimes you have to rock the boat, and that upsets those who want the status quo, but our members expect this," Fain said.

> "We encourage the Supervisors to investigate any complaints brought to their offices, because we know what they will find: UAW leadership is committed to serving its members and running a union democracy. We are focused on winning record contracts, growing our union, and fighting for social and economic justice on and off the job."

Whatever Biden's role in this smear, endorsing political candidates and supporting the Trump/Biden trade war obviously will not prevent these outrageous government attacks on the UAW and the growing trade union movement.

The Big Three, Big Oil, Wall Street, the whole imperialist establishment is not willing to produce the electric vehicles that the workers and oppressed communities can afford and are certainly unwilling to fully compensate the workers to produce them.

Time for change

So, to continue to fight for high-paying jobs for workers to produce low-price EVs essential to reduce carbon emissions, the union movement should consider a different view of socialist China and its vast "green energy" capabilities, as opposed to the billionaire class's fixation on economic and social hegemony, its trade war and its push towards a military conflict and regime change, as well as its campaign to squeeze everything it can out of our class here.

The Chinese company BYD does have a factory in the U.S. in Los Angeles where it produces electric buses. Unlike their European counterparts in anti-union southern states, the BYD plant's 700 workers are members of the Sheet Metal Air, Rail, and Transportation Workers Union (SMART), Local 105.

Since U.S. auto companies are only interested in building fewer and more expensive EVs, costing tens of thousands of dollars more than their gasoline equivalents, the UAW is certainly entitled to call on Biden to invite Chinese auto companies to open plants in this country to produce the same low price high quality EVs they currently produce in China, but only if they pledge to recognize the UAW as the representative of the workers.

The union can also call for the same for Chinese battery companies. BYD, which produces new sodium batteries that are much cheaper and more environmentally "friendly" than lithium batteries, safer from fire, not degraded by low or high temperatures, do not require cobalt and other rare metals, and are far easier to recycle, could be invited to open facilities in the U.S.

Large sodium batteries used to store solar panel and wind turbine power during nighttime and calm winds are already being produced in China. Soda ash, which the U.S. has an abundance of, could be a sodium source far cheaper than lithium, of which the U.S. has little supply.

Some could even be exported back to China.

Inviting these companies to open such battery plants in this country could be a huge gain for both the union and environmental movement and link the two movements together. Finally, it could convert the dangerous ruling class spawned hostility towards China into genuine working-class solidarity.

Chris Fry is a Chrysler retiree and former member of UAW Local 51. He worked on the pre-final line as an assembler at Chrysler Lynch Road Assembly before the company shut down the plant.

Source: Fighting Words

Stephen Millies | Sept. 5, 2022

Why China isn't capitalist

Wall Street and the Pentagon view the People's Republic of China as their number one enemy. China is the target of U.S. imperialism's "Pivot to Asia."

China's economy may already be larger than the United States. The American Enterprise Institute – one of the best-known capitalist think tanks – admits China surpassed the U.S. as the world's biggest manufacturer back in 2010.

That's historically significant. Factories in the United States exceeded Britain's production in the 1890s.

China is now the "workshop of the world." In 2021, China built nearly 17 million more motor vehicles than the U.S.

This tremendous economic growth is the result of China's socialist revolution. It's not just a matter of China making more than a billion tons of steel a year or having more miles of high-speed rail than the rest of the world.

When Mao Zedong declared "China has stood up" in 1949 and the People's Republic of China was born, Chinese people lived to be, on average, just 36 years old.

By 2022 life expectancy had more than doubled to reach 77.3 years. That's a longer lifespan than in the United States.

Despite these tremendous gains, some communists and revolutionaries contend that capitalism has been restored in the People's Republic of China. They point to the 606 billionaires in China, including 67 in Hong Kong.

The capitalist world market

The People's Republic of China is entangled in the capitalist world market. Almost $2.5 trillion in foreign direct investment has poured into China since 1992.

This represents millions of Chinese workers being exploited by foreign capitalists. For example, in 2021, General Motors made 2.9 million cars in China.

That's almost 700,000 more vehicles than it sold in the U.S. Tesla is investing $7.5 billion in its Shanghai "gigafactory."

Unlike China before liberation, none of this investment is colonial in character. Foreign corporations have to share technology and know-how. Elon Musk ignored California's safety regulations during the height of the COVID-19 pandemic, but he has to follow Chinese laws.

Mistakes shouldn't be repeated

Decades ago, many revolutionaries had already considered the Soviet Union to be capitalist.

Mikhail Gorbachev – who opened the door to capitalist restoration – didn't come out of nowhere. He rose in the bureaucracy under both Khrushchev and Brezhnev.

There were hundreds of thousands of Gorbachevs in the Soviet government and Communist Party. They were supporters of Gorbachev's anti-Marxist "new thinking" that sneered at the class struggle. These elements shared Gorbachev's illusions about U.S. imperialism and capitalist society in general.

Most of the "oligarchs" came from their ranks. They stole trillions of dollars worth of socialist property that workers and peasant farmers had built over a dozen five-year plans.

Aided the liberation of Angola, Namibia

Yet as late as 1988, Soviet-built MiG-25 jet fighters gave the People's Armed Forces of Liberation of Angola air superiority in the crucial battle of Cuito Cuanavale. A coalition of liberation forces decisively defeated the apartheid army from South Africa, backed by the Pentagon.

These included the People's Liberation Army of Namibia (PLAN), the armed wing of the South West Africa People's Organization (SWAPO); uMkhonto we Sizwe (MK), the armed section of the African National Congress (ANC), and the Revolutionary Armed Forces of Cuba. Also present were military advisers from the Socialist Republic of Vietnam and the Soviet Union.

Less than two years after this battle, Nelson Mandela walked out of prison on Feb. 11, 1990.

Apartheid South Africa first invaded the newly independent People's Republic of Angola in 1975. Africa called, and Cuba answered. Cuban volunteers shed their blood beside their African comrades.

Critics of the Soviet leadership could see for themselves which side of the world the Soviet Union and its allies were on.

It's been over 30 years since socialism was tragically overthrown in the Soviet Union. This was a greater defeat for workers and oppressed people everywhere than Hitler crushing the German working class.

To have written off Soviet socialism in the decades before Gorbachev rose to power confused revolutionaries. It disarmed communists when the real counter-revolutionary threat appeared.

Socialism vs. COVID

Those that claimed that the Soviet Union was already capitalist 50 or 60 years ago apparently didn't understand that capitalism can't function without a huge body of unemployed workers. Frederick Engels, the co-thinker of Karl Marx, called jobless workers the industrial reserve army.

Capitalists know this well. Sam Insull – whose crooked Midwestern utility empire collapsed in the Great Depression – declared that "the greatest aid to the efficiency of labor is a long line of men waiting at the gate." Meaning women and men desperately seeking a job.

But there was no industrial reserve army in the Soviet Union. Instead, the country suffered from a labor shortage.

This was one of the features of Soviet society that made it incompatible with capitalism. The Soviet economy was planned. A state monopoly of foreign trade kept the International Monetary Fund and the World Bank at bay.

In contrast to the Soviet Union, millions of workers in the People's Republic of China are without a job. The unemployment rate for youth between 16 and 24 years old reached 19.9% in July.

Particularly affected are the record number of 10.75 million college graduates. Before liberation in 1949, there were only 117,000 college students in China.

A big reason for the lack of hiring has been the anti-COVID actions that socialist China took. The capitalist media attacked these absolutely necessary health measures.

Huge cities like Beijing and Shanghai were temporarily closed. Unarmed socialist police in Wuhan delivered meals to people in their homes.

This was a clear contest between capitalism and socialism. In the U.S., 1,046,243 people have died from COVID-19 as of Sept. 1.

Meanwhile, 14,922 people died in the People's Republic of China, which has over a billion more people than the United States. (China's total includes 9,701 people who died in the capitalist Special Administrative Region of Hong Kong.)

No capitalist government on earth could have done what socialist China did in fighting the pandemic. Banksters and billionaires wouldn't have allowed it. Profits are more precious than life to billionaires and their media stooges.

John Tyson (chicken billionaire) and other dead-animal capitalists got Trump to issue an executive order keeping the meatpacking plants open and shielding themselves from lawsuits. As a result, over 59,000 meatpacking workers caught the virus, and 269 died.

Kept on a leash

China has a sizeable capitalist class, with 606 billionaires forming its crest. These capitalists are kept on a leash.

Liu Han's $6 billion stash didn't prevent him from being executed in 2015. A millionaire (much less a billionaire) has never been executed in the United States.

A handful of banks play a dominant role over the U.S. government. The Communist Party of China runs China's banks.

The commanding heights of China's economy are controlled by the Communist Party. While production has stagnated in the imperialist countries, China's steel production leaped from 400 million tons in 2007 to over a billion tons today.

You can't explain China's fantastic economic growth except by admitting there's some other social system than capitalism in charge.

If socialism had been overthrown in China, there would be no need for a separate regime for capitalist Hong Kong, which has its own currency. China liberated Hong Kong from British colonialism in 1997.

After the Soviet Union was destroyed, Wall Street's next target was China. But, to many in the military-industrial complex, NATO's 78 days of bombing Yugoslavia was a poor substitute.

Their frustration was behind the deliberate bombing of the Chinese embassy in Belgrade.

NATO's war against Yugoslavia was a class war. Despite all the concessions that Tito had made to imperialism, what remained of Yugoslavia in 1999 was socialist in class character.

Sometimes retreats are absolutely necessary. For example, the Long March was a glorious retreat that saved the Communist Party of China from being destroyed.

Mao Zedong argued for the Red Army to take the Long March to escape encirclement. Lenin and the Bolsheviks had to make a sharp economic retreat in the early 1920s by launching NEP, the New Economic Policy.

Karl Marx contemplated that following a socialist revolution, the working class might have to "buy off the band" of well-to-do elements.

Confronted by world imperialism, the People's Republic of China has allowed both foreign and domestic capital to flourish. It was a case of bending instead of being broken.

Growth of China's working class

While the capitalist class has grown in China, much more spectacular has been the growth of the working class.

The Chinese Revolution's biggest problem was the small number of workers in the country. In 1949, workers were perhaps 1% of the population.

Today the working class in the People's Republic of China is hundreds of millions strong. Thousands of strikes occur against private capitalists.

Chinese workers credit communism for China's tremendous advances in health and economic growth. The social weight of the working class has been responsible for China's extensive reforms in health care and education over the last 20 years.

Those who claim that a counter-revolution has taken place in China should show when this overthrow occurred. Comrade Mao Zedong famously wrote that a revolution is not a dinner party.

A counter-revolution is far bloodier. The events following Mao's death couldn't have changed China's class character.

Just as a rising class needs to smash the state machine of the old ruling class – as was done in the French and Bolshevik revolutions – so would a counter-revolution need to smash the apparatus built by the Chinese Revolution. That hasn't happened.

To claim that the concessions made to capitalists over the last 45 years amount to overthrowing the Chinese Revolution is reformism in reverse.

There are many more chapters to be written in the Chinese Revolution. The working class in the People's Republic of China – which includes millions of workers from minority nationalities like the Uyghurs and Tibetans – will have the last word.

Long live the Chinese Revolution!

No war on
CHINA

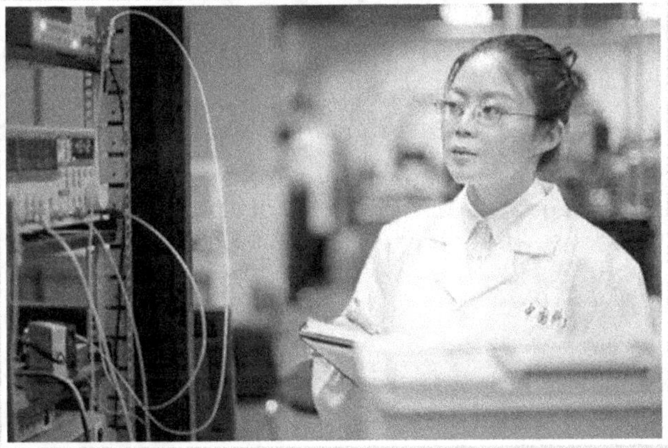

Peng Xinhua, professor of Physical Sciences at the University of Science and Technology of China, does research in quantum physics, atomic, molecular and optical physics, and experimental physics, and holds the world record for the maximum number of the quantum factoring algorithm.

hainei.org

The sanctions are part of the U.S. campaign to stifle China's development of the latest version of data-transmission technology known as 5G.

Photo: China Daily

Fred Goldstein | August 6, 2019

The new Cold War against China

During the Cold War and the struggle that put the USSR and China on one side and imperialism headed by Washington on the other side, revolutionaries used to characterize the conflict as a class war between two irreconcilable social systems.

There was the socialist camp, based upon socialized property, economic planning for human needs, and the government monopoly of foreign trade on the USSR-China side, and capitalism, a system of production for profit, on the other.

That the two systems were irreconcilable was at the bottom of the conflict dubbed the Cold War. In light of the current sharpening economic, diplomatic, political, and military conflict between U.S. imperialism and the People's Republic of China (PRC), it is time to revive the concepts that were applied during the height of the Cold War.

The conflict between imperialist capitalism, headed by Washington, Wall Street, and the Pentagon, and the Chinese socialist economic system, which has state-owned industry at its core and planned economic guidance, is becoming much sharper, and imperialism is growing more openly hostile.

U.S. imperialism's long-standing effort to overthrow socialism in China, Chinese capitalism notwithstanding, has been concealed beneath sugary bourgeois phrases about so-called "common interests" and "economic collaboration." But this kind of talk is coming to an end.

Washington's first campaign to overthrow China — 1949-1975

This struggle has been ongoing since 1949 when the Chinese Red Army drove U.S. puppet Chiang Kai-shek and his nationalist army from the mainland as it retreated to Taiwan under the protection of the Pentagon.

The conflict continued through the Korean War when Gen. Douglas MacArthur and the U.S. high command drove the U.S. troops to the Chinese border and threatened atomic war. Only the defeat of the U.S. military by the heroic Korean people under the leadership of Kim Il Sung, with the aid of the Chinese Red Army, stopped the U.S. invasion of China.

The struggle further continued with the U.S. war against Vietnam. The war's strategic goal was to overthrow the socialist government of Vietnam in the north and drive to the border of China to complete the military encirclement of the PRC. Only the world-historic efforts of the Vietnamese people under the leadership of Ho Chi Minh stopped the Pentagon in its tracks.

The Pentagon's plans for military conquest failed

With the rise of Deng Xiaoping and the opening up of China to foreign investment beginning in December 1978,

Wall Street began to reevaluate its strategy. The U.S. ruling class began to take advantage of the opening up of China to foreign investment and the permission for private capitalism to function, which could both enrich U.S. corporations in the massive Chinese market and, at the same time, penetrate the Chinese economy with a long-range view to overturning socialism.

U.S. multinational corporations set up operations in China, hiring millions of low-wage Chinese workers who flocked to the coastal cities from the rural areas. These operations were part of a broader effort by the U.S. capitalists to set up low-wage global supply chains that integrated the Chinese economy into the world capitalist market. The U.S.'s recent sharp turn aimed at breaking up this economic integration with the Chinese economy, including the witch hunt against Chinese scientists and the U.S. Navy's aggressive behavior in the South China Sea (called the Eastern Sea by Vietnam), is an admission that the economic phase of the U.S. attempt to bring counterrevolution to China has failed.

China is now a growing counterweight to Washington in international economics, high technology, diplomacy, and regional military might in the Pacific, which the Pentagon has always considered to be a "U.S. lake" ruled by the Seventh Fleet.

The attack on Huawei

A dramatic illustration of the developing antagonisms is the way the U.S. had Meng Wanzhou, the deputy chairwoman and chief financial officer of Huawei, arrested in Canada

for supposed violations of U.S. sanctions against Iran —
an outrageous example of imperialism exercising extra-
territoriality. The Trump administration has also leveled
sanctions against Huawei electronics, the world's largest
supplier of high-tech operating systems in the world. Huawei employs 180,000 workers and is the second largest cell
phone manufacturer in the world after the South Korean-
based Samsung.

The sanctions are part of the U.S. campaign to stifle
China's development of the latest version of data-transmission technology known as Fifth Generation or 5G.

The Trump administration has barred U.S. companies
from selling supplies to Huawei, which has been using Google's Android operating system for its equipment and Microsoft for its laptop products — both U.S.-based companies.
Huawei is contesting the U.S. ban in court.

Meanwhile, as a backup plan in case Washington bans
all access to Android and Microsoft, Huawei has quietly
spent years building up an operating system of its own.
Huawei developed its alternative operating system after a
2012 finding by Washington that Huawei and ZTE, another
Chinese giant cell phone maker, were in criminal violation
of U.S. "national security." ZTE was forced to shut down for
four months. (South China Morning Post, March 24, 2019)

But the conflict is about more than just Huawei and ZTE.

The new 'red scare' in Washington

The New York Times of July 20, 2019, carried a front-page
article entitled "The New Red Scare in Washington." A few
excerpts give the flavor:

"In a ballroom across from the Capitol building, an unlikely group of military hawks, populist crusaders, Chinese Muslim freedom fighters, and followers of the Falun Gong has been meeting to warn anyone who will listen that China poses an existential threat to the United States that will not end until the Communist Party is overthrown.

"If the warnings sound straight out of the Cold War, they are. The Committee on the Present Danger, a long-defunct group that campaigned against the dangers of the Soviet Union in the 1970s and 1980s, has recently been revived with the help of Stephen K. Bannon, the president's former chief strategist, to warn against the dangers of China.

"Once dismissed as xenophobes and fringe elements, the group's members are finding their views increasingly embraced in President Trump's Washington, where skepticism and mistrust of China have taken hold. Fear of China has spread across the government, from the White House to Congress to federal agencies."

The Trump administration has opened up a tariff war against the PRC, imposing a 25-percent tariff on $250 billion worth of Chinese exports and threatening tariffs on another $300 billion. But there is much more to Washington's campaign than just tariffs.

The FBI and officials from the NSC (National Security Council) have been conducting a witch hunt, continues the Times article, "particularly at universities and research institutions. Officials from the FBI and the National Security Council have been dispatched to Ivy League universities to warn administrators to be vigilant against Chinese students."

And according to the Times, there are concerns that this witch hunt "is stoking a new red scare, fueling discrimination against students, scientists and companies with ties to China and risking the collapse of a fraught but deeply enmeshed trade relationship between the world's two largest economies." (New York Times, July 20, 2019)

FBI criminalizes cancer research

According to a major article in the June 13, 2019, Bloomberg News, "Ways of working that have long been encouraged by the NIH [National Institutes of Health] and many research institutions, particularly MD Anderson [a major cancer treatment center and research institute in Houston], are now quasi-criminalized, with FBI agents reading private emails, stopping Chinese scientists at airports, and visiting people's homes to ask about their loyalty.

"Xifeng Wu, who has been investigated by the FBI, joined MD Anderson while in graduate school and gained renown for creating several so-called study cohorts with data amassed from hundreds of thousands of patients in Asia and the U.S. The cohorts, which combine patient histories with personal biomarkers such as DNA characteristics and treatment descriptions, outcomes, and even lifestyle habits, are a gold mine for researchers.

"She was branded an oncological double agent."

The underlying accusation against Chinese scientists in the U.S. is that their research can lead to patentable medicines or cures, which in turn can be sold at enormous profits.

The Bloomberg article continues, "In recent decades, cancer research has become increasingly globalized, with scientists around the world pooling data and ideas to jointly study a disease that kills almost 10 million people a year. International collaborations are an intrinsic part of the U.S. National Cancer Institute's Moonshot program, the government's $1 billion blitz to double the pace of treatment discoveries by 2022. One of the program's tag lines is: 'Cancer knows no borders.'

"Except, it turns out, the borders around China. In January, Wu, an award-winning epidemiologist and naturalized American citizen, quietly stepped down as director of the Center for Public Health and Translational Genomics at the University of Texas MD Anderson Cancer Center after a three-month investigation into her professional ties in China. Wu's resignation, and the departures in recent months of three other top Chinese-American scientists from Houston-based MD Anderson, stem from a Trump administration drive to counter Chinese influence at U.S. research institutions. … The collateral effect, however, is to stymie basic science, the foundational research that underlies new medical treatments. Everything is commodified in the economic cold war with China, including the struggle to find a cure for cancer."

Big surprise. A world-famous Chinese epidemiologist trying to find a cure for cancer collaborates with scientists in China!

Looking for the 'reformers' and the counterrevolution

For decades, the Chinese Communist Party has had changes of leadership every five years. These changes have been stable and managed peacefully. With each changeover, so-called "China experts" in the State Department in Washington think tanks and U.S. universities have predicted the coming to power of a new "reformist" wing that will deepen capitalist reforms and lay the basis for an eventual full-scale capitalist counterrevolution.

To be sure, there has been a steady erosion of China's socialist institutions. The "iron rice bowl" which guaranteed a living to Chinese workers, has been eliminated in private enterprises. Numerous state factories and enterprises have been sold off to the detriment of the workers, and in the rural areas, land was decollectivized.

One of the biggest setbacks for socialism in China and one which truly gladdened the hearts of the prophets of counterrevolution, was the decision by the Jiang Jemin CPC leadership to allow capitalists into the Communist Party of China in 2001.

As the New York Times wrote at the time, "This decision raises the possibility of Communists co-opting capitalists — or of capitalists co-opting the party." (New York Times, Aug. 13, 2001) It was the latter part that the capitalist class has been looking forward to and striving for with fervent anticipation for almost four decades.

But on balance, this capitalist takeover has not material-ized. Chinese socialism, despite the capitalist inroads into the economy, has proved far more durable than Washing-ton ever imagined.

And, under the Xi Jinping leadership, the counterrevolu-tion seems to be getting further and further away. It is not that Xi Jinping has become a revolutionary internationalist and a champion of proletarian control. However, it has be-come apparent that China's status in the world is completely connected to its social and economic planning.

China's planning and state enterprises overcame the 2007-2009 world capitalist crisis

Without state planning in the economy, China might have been dragged down by the 2007-2009 economic crisis. In June 2013, this author wrote an article entitled "Marxism and the Social Character of China." Here are some excerpts:

"More than 20 million Chinese workers lost their jobs in a very short time. So what did the Chinese government do?"

The article quoted Nicholas Lardy, a bourgeois China expert from the prestigious Peterson Institute for International Economics and no friend of China. (The full article by Lardy can be found in "Sustaining China's Economic Growth after the Global Financial Crisis," Kindle Locations 664-666, Peterson Institute for International Economics.)

Lardy described how "consumption in China actually grew during the crisis of 2008-09, wages went up, and the government created enough jobs to compensate for the lay-offs caused by the global crisis," this author's emphasis.

Lardy continued: "In a year in which GDP expansion [in China] was the slowest in almost a decade, how could consumption growth in 2009 have been so strong in relative terms? How could this happen at a time when employment in export-oriented industries was collapsing, with a survey conducted by the Ministry of Agriculture reporting the loss of 20 million jobs in export manufacturing centers along the southeast coast, notably in Guangdong Province? The relatively strong growth of consumption in 2009 is explained by several factors.

"First, the boom in investment, particularly in construction activities, appears to have generated additional employment sufficient to offset a very large portion of the job losses in the export sector. For the year as a whole the Chinese economy created 11.02 million jobs in urban areas, very nearly matching the 11.13 million urban jobs created in 2008.

"Second, while the growth of employment slowed slightly, wages continued to rise. In nominal terms, wages in the formal sector rose 12 percent, a few percentage points below the average of the previous five years (National Bureau of Statistics of China 2010f, 131). In real terms, the increase was almost 13 percent.

"Third, the government continued its programs of increasing payments to those drawing pensions and raising transfer payments to China's lowest-income residents. Monthly pension payments for enterprise retirees increased by RMB120, or 10 percent, in January 2009, substantially more than the 5.9 percent increase in consumer prices in 2008. This raised the total payments to retirees by about RMB75 billion. The Ministry of Civil Affairs raised transfer payments to about 70 million of China's lowest-income citizens by a third, for an increase of RMB20 billion in 2009 (Ministry of Civil Affairs 2010)."

Lardy further explained that the Ministry of Railroads introduced eight specific plans to be completed in 2020 to be implemented in the crisis.

According to Lardy, the World Bank called it "perhaps the biggest single planned program of passenger rail investment there has ever been in one country." In addition, ultrahigh-voltage grid projects were undertaken, among other advances.

Socialist structures reversed collapse

So income went up, consumption went up, and unemployment was overcome in China — all while the capitalist world was still mired in mass unemployment, austerity, recession, stagnation, slow growth and increasing poverty, and still is to a large extent.

The reversal of the effects of the crisis in China is the direct result of national planning, state-owned enterprises, state-owned banking and the policy decisions of the Chinese Communist Party.

There was a crisis in China, and it was caused by the world capitalist crisis. The question was which principle would prevail in the face of mass unemployment — the rational, humane principle of planning or the ruthless capitalist market. In China, the planning principle, the conscious element, took precedence over the anarchy of production brought about by the laws of the market and the law of labor value in capitalist countries.

Socialism and China's standing in the world

China has lifted hundreds of millions of people out of poverty. According to a United Nations report, China alone is responsible for the global decline in poverty. China's universities have graduated millions of engineers, scientists, and technicians and have allowed millions of peasants to enter the modern world.

Made in China 2025

In 2015, Xi Jinping and the Chinese CP leadership laid out the equivalent of a ten-year plan to take China to a higher level of technology and productivity in the struggle to modernize the country.

Xi announced a long-range industrial policy backed by hundreds of billions of dollars in both state and private investment to revitalize China. It is named "Made in China 2025" or "MIC25." It is an ambitious project requiring local, regional, and national coordination and participation.

The Mercator Institute for Economics (MERICS) is one of the most authoritative German think tanks on China. It wrote a major report on MIC25 on Feb. 7, 2019. According to MERICS, "The MIC25 program is here to stay and, just like the GDP targets of the past, represents the CCP's official marching orders for an ambitious industrial upgrading. Capitalist economies around the globe will have to face this strategic offensive.

"The tables have already started to turn: Today, China is setting the pace in many emerging technologies — and watches as the world tries to keep pace."

The MERICS report continues, "China has forged ahead in fields such as next-generation IT (companies like Huawei and ZTE are set to gain global dominance in the rollout of 5G networks), high-speed railways, and ultra-high voltage electricity transmissions. More than 530 smart manufacturing industrial parks have popped up in China. Many focus on big data (21 percent), new materials (17 percent), and cloud computing (13 percent). Recently, green manufacturing and the creation of an "Industrial Internet" were given special emphasis in policy documents, underpinning President Xi Jinping's vision of creating an 'ecological civilization' that thrives on sustainable development.

"China has also secured a strong position in areas such as Artificial Intelligence (AI), new energy and intelligent connected vehicles. …

"Chinese state-owned enterprises (SOEs) continue to play a critical role for the development of strategic industries and high-tech equipment associated with MIC25. In so-called key industries like telecommunications, ship building, aviation and high-speed railways, SOEs still have a revenue share of around 83 percent. In what the Chinese government has identified as pillar industries (for instance electronics, equipment manufacturing, or automotive) it amounts to 45 percent."

Breakup of U.S.-China relationship inevitable

The tariff war between the U.S. and China has been going back and forth. It may or may not be resolved for now or may end up in a compromise. The Pentagon's provocations in the South China Sea and the Pacific are unlikely to subside. The witch hunt against Chinese scientists is gaining momentum.

The U.S. has just appropriated $2.2 billion for arms to Taiwan. National Security Adviser and war hawk John Bolton recently made a trip to Taiwan. The president of Taiwan, Tsai Ing-wen, made a recent stopover in the U.S. on the way to the Caribbean and is scheduled to make another one on the way back.

All these measures indicate the end of the rapprochement between Beijing and Washington. This breakup between the two powers is not just the doing of Donald Trump. It flows from the growing fear of the predominant sections of the U.S. ruling class that the gamble they took in trying to overthrow Chinese socialism from within has failed, just as the previous military aggression from 1949 to 1975 also failed.

High technology is the key to the future

Since as far back as the end of the 18th century, the U.S. capitalist class has always coveted the Chinese market. The giant capitalist monopolies went charging in to get joint agreements, low wages, cheap exports, and big superprofits when China "opened up" at the end of the 1970s.

But the stronger the socialist core of the PRC becomes, the more weight it carries in the world, and, above all, the stronger China becomes technologically, the more Wall Street fears for its economic dominance and the more the Pentagon fears for its military dominance.

The example of the stifling of international collaboration on cancer research is a demonstration of how global cooperation is essential not only to curing disease but also to the development of society as a whole. International cooperation is needed to reverse the climate disaster wrought by private property — none of this can be carried out within the framework of private property and the profit system. Only the destruction of capitalism can bring about the liberation of humanity.

Marxism asserts that society advances through the development of the productive forces from primary communism to slavery, feudalism, and capitalism. Marx wrote: "The hand-mill gives you society with the feudal lord; the steam-mill society with the industrial capitalist." ("The Poverty of Philosophy," 1847) And now the revolution in high technology lays the basis for international socialism.

The bourgeoisie knows that the society that can advance technology to the highest degree will be triumphant in shaping the future. This is why imperialism, headed by the U.S., imposed the strictest blockade of the flow of technology to the Soviet Union, as well as the Eastern Bloc and China. This was done by COCOM, an informal organization of all the imperialist countries, which was created in 1949 and headquartered in Paris.

The main targets were the USSR and the more industrialized socialist countries, such as the German Democratic Republic, the Czech Republic, etc. Detailed lists were drawn up of some 1,500 technological items that were forbidden to export to these countries.

Marx explained that developed socialist relations depend upon a high degree of the productivity of labor and the resulting abundance available to the population ("Critique of the Gotha Program," 1875).

However, as Lenin noted, the chain of imperialism broke at its weakest link in Russia — that is, the revolution was successful in the poorest, most backward capitalist country. The result was that an advanced social system was established on an insufficient material foundation. This gave rise to many, many contradictions. The countries that revolutionaries correctly called socialist were, in fact, really aspiring to socialism. Their revolutions laid the foundations for socialism. But imperialist blockade, war, and subversion never allowed them to freely develop their social systems.

The great leap forward in technology in China today has the potential of raising the productivity of labor and strengthening the socialist foundations. It is this great leap forward that is fueling the "new cold war" with China and the real threat of a hot war.

Taiwan National Police Agency Special Operations force in Taipei, Oct. 9, 2020.

Gary Wilson | Oct. 14, 2021

Washington escalates:
U.S. special forces secretly operating for past year in Taiwan

Unless the U.S. government promptly removes its military forces from China's Taiwan province, China may send in its own military force to defend its territory, declared an Oct. 8 editorial in Global Times, the Communist Party of China's daily newspaper.

Global Times explains: "We must resolutely define the deployment of U.S. troops in Taiwan as an 'invasion.' The mainland has the right to carry out military strikes against them at any time. We will not make any promises over their safety. Once a war breaks out in the Taiwan Straits, those U.S. military personnel will be the first to be eliminated. Through such a declaration, we must make Washington understand that it is playing a dangerous game that is destined to draw fire onto itself and it is risking the lives of young U.S. soldiers."

On Oct. 7, the Wall Street Journal reported that about two dozen U.S. special operations and support troops were "secretly operating in Taiwan to train military forces there for at least a year." The Global Times points out that "since the

U.S. has exposed the news through anonymous officials, it has taken a step forward to undermine, from covertly to semi-overtly, the key conditions for the establishment of diplomatic relations between the Chinese mainland and the U.S."

The U.S. government officially recognizes that Taiwan is a province of China, not a separate nation. Therefore, what the Biden administration is now doing — secretly sending special forces into the Chinese province — is in violation of both U.S. and international law.

Taiwan is a crucial issue. The struggle over Taiwan, always considered to be a province of China, has been ongoing since 1949, when the Chinese People's Liberation Army drove U.S. puppet Chiang Kai-shek and his Nationalist Army from the mainland as it retreated to Taiwan under the protection of the Pentagon.

Shanghai Communiqué: One China

The U.S. agreed to surrender the Chinese province of Taiwan, as promised in the Shanghai Communiqué, on Feb. 28, 1972.

The U.S. signed a promise that "The United States acknowledges that all Chinese on either side of the Taiwan Strait maintain there is but one China and that Taiwan is a part of China. The United States Government does not challenge that position. It reaffirms its interest in a peaceful settlement of the Taiwan question by the Chinese themselves."

The Trump administration moved toward dropping most of the long-standing policies toward China and Taiwan, even suggesting the possibility of granting Taiwan official recognition and an embassy in Washington.

The Biden administration has not changed any of the Trump policies toward China.

A Democratic congresswoman, Rep. Elaine Luria, in an op-ed published in the Washington Post Oct. 11, "Congress must untie Biden's hands on Taiwan," called for an act that would allow the president to bypass Congress to declare war on China.

The Stars and Stripes daily newspaper that's issued from the Pentagon headlined Oct. 12: "Retired Marine colonel says U.S. should weigh nuclear war with China over Taiwan."

Ruling class behind anti-China campaign

Has the rapprochement between Washington and Beijing, as represented by the Shanghai Communiqué, ended?

This breakup is not just the doing of Donald Trump or Joe Biden. It flows from the fear of the predominant sections of the U.S. ruling class that the attempt to overthrow Chinese socialism from within has failed, just as the previous military aggression from 1949 to 1975 also failed.

In the 1970s when China "opened up," the giant capitalist monopolies went charging into the Chinese markets. But the strong socialist core of the People's Republic of China has held on. And the stronger China becomes, the more Wall Street fears for its economic dominance and the more the Pentagon fears for its military dominance.

On Feb. 25, China's President Xi Jinping announced that 853 million Chinese people have lifted themselves out of poverty since 1981 thanks to large-scale interventions from both the Chinese state and the Communist Party of China.

China's technological and economic strength — as well as its remarkable response to the coronavirus (4,636 total deaths compared to more than 718,000 in the U.S.) — has raised a new respect for socialism.

U.S. ruling class hostility to China's struggle to build a socialist society is behind the New Cold War and the real threat of hot war.

Gary Wilson | Nov. 3, 2021

Biden targets China: Turning Taiwan into a military outpost

The Guardian reports that U.S. Secretary of State Antony Blinken threatened a U.S. military buildup in Taiwan in a "side meeting" at the G20 summit in Rome on Oct. 31.

The Guardian added that Blinken's threat "came a week after Biden said the U.S. may support Taiwan's independence militarily and Blinken called for Taiwan to be recognized within U.N. institutions."

On Oct. 7, the Wall Street Journal reported that about two dozen U.S. special operations and support troops were "secretly operating in Taiwan to train military forces there for at least a year."

The U.S. government officially recognizes that Taiwan is a province of China, not a separate nation. By a 1979 agreement, the U.S. promised to remove all military personnel from Taiwan.

Therefore, what the Biden administration is now doing — secretly sending military forces into the Chinese province — is in violation of both U.S. and international law.

The Chinese province of Taiwan, once a colony of Japan, now calls itself the Republic of China. The U.S. government decided to designate Taiwan as the government of all China after Mao Zedong proclaimed the People's Republic of China on Oct. 1, 1949. Taiwan was never the capital of China, but it has been part of China for millennia.

To the people of China, Blinken probably sounds like a reminder of the European and Japanese colonialists of the 19th century who had seized Taiwan and other parts of China and used military force to "protect" their possessions.

Century of colonialism

In China it's known as the "century of humiliation": the years of dismemberment and subjugation by the European and Japanese imperialists from 1839 to 1949.

The First Opium War began in 1839. Britain grew opium in India and sold it in China, using the profits to purchase Chinese goods, including porcelain, silk and tea. When the Qing government in China tried to stop the importation of opium, Britain launched the "Opium War" to keep the drug flowing into China.

In the century of colonialism, China was fractured, with Outer Manchuria, parts of Northwest China and Sakhalin seized by Tsarist Russia; Jiaozhou Bay by Germany; Hong Kong and Tibet by Britain; Macau by Portugal; Zhanjiang by France; and Taiwan by Japan.

Japan was a relative latecomer to the imperialist club. Taiwan was its first colony. Japanese rule of Taiwan lasted from 1895 to the end of World War II in August 1945.

At the end of the war in 1945, the U.S. military, led by General Douglas MacArthur, occupied Japan and took charge of Japan's colonies, particularly Korea and Taiwan. The U.S. military forces put Taiwan under the administrative control of the Kuomintang-led Republic of China, with

Chiang Kai-Shek at the head. This was a confirmation that Taiwan was a part of China.

Retrocession Day is the name given to the annual observance and former public holiday in Taiwan to commemorate the end of Japanese rule of Taiwan, and the retrocession ("return") of Taiwan to the Republic of China on Oct. 25, 1945.

From the end of World War II in 1945 to 1949, a war of liberation was fought by the People's Liberation Army and the Communist Party of China, which led to the founding of the People's Republic of China. In 1949, Chiang Kai-Shek and the Kuomintang army fled to Taiwan under U.S. military protection.

The U.S. strongly supported the Kuomintang forces against the Chinese Revolution. The Kuomintang received $4.43 billion from the U.S., most of it military aid, according to William Blum in his book "Killing Hope."

In June 1950, when the U.S. launched its war on Korea, the U.S. government also sent the Seventh Fleet into the Taiwan Strait with the Chinese mainland as its target. At the time, MacArthur wanted to use nuclear weapons against China — in an interview he said he would have dropped "30 or so atomic bombs." MacArthur also wanted to use Chiang Kai-Shek's forces in Taiwan to invade the mainland.

In 1949, Chiang Kai-Shek and the Kuomintang had declared martial law in Taiwan, imposing a brutal military regime that wasn't lifted until 1987. During these decades of martial law, some 140,000 Taiwanese were arrested, tortured and imprisoned, according to a 2008 report by the Executive Yuan (government) of Taiwan. Some 4,000 people were executed.

Secret U.S. military operations

In the early 1950s, a secret group of U.S. military "advisers," led by retired Adm. Charles M. Cooke, former commander of the Seventh Fleet, launched covert military operations in Taiwan to prop up the unpopular and weak Kuomintang regime.

The struggle over Taiwan has continued to this day.

After the victory of the Chinese Revolution and the formation of the People's Republic of China, Washington proclaimed the military dictatorship in Taiwan to be the "Republic of China" and the government of all China. The Taiwan military regime was even given China's seat in the imperialist-dominated United Nations!

The U.S. didn't change this policy until 1972, when it was losing the Vietnam War.

In the 1972 Shanghai Communiqué, the U.S. agreed "that all Chinese on either side of the Taiwan Strait maintain there is but one China and that Taiwan is a part of China. The United States Government does not challenge that position. It reaffirms its interest in a peaceful settlement of the Taiwan question by the Chinese themselves."

This was followed by the Normalization Communiqué of 1979, with the U.S. formally ending recognition of the "Republic of China" and agreeing to withdraw all U.S. military personnel from Taiwan.

However, the U.S. never stopped arms sales to Taiwan. These arms sales are supposed to be public and of a "defensive nature" only. The list of U.S. arms sales is publicly available on the Federal Register. Secret arms sales or operations are forbidden, which is what makes the Biden administration's secret deployment of military special operations trainers a clear escalation of hostilities.

Following the 1979 communiqué, U.S. arms sales to Taiwan have increased every year. In 2020, the Pentagon announced more than $1.8 billion in arms to Taiwan, including 135 precision-guided cruise missiles and rocket launchers.

Separatists vs. Indigenous Taiwanese

Following the end of martial law in 1987, a new political party emerged in Taiwan to challenge the Kuomintang. The Democratic Progressive Party (DPP) is a Taiwanese nationalist party and currently controls the presidency and the Legislative Yuan. The Kuomintang remains as the second major party in Taiwan.

While the Kuomintang agrees there is only one China and opposes Taiwanese "independence," the DPP claims Taiwan to be a separate nation. The Kuomintang is based on the mainland Chinese population that came with Chiang Kai-Shek's military occupation force; the DPP is led by the Chinese who had preceded them.

Over 95% of Taiwan's population of 23.4 million consists of Han Chinese, whose traditional ancestral homes are in the southern part of Fujian, China.

The Indigenous peoples in Taiwan are Austronesian Taiwanese, who make up 2.3% of the total population. The DPP does not represent the Indigenous population and, in fact, is considered to be hostile to the Indigenous Taiwanese.

In 2016, during a legislative committee meeting, a DPP legislator used a racist, anti-Indigenous slur in responding to a request made by Indigenous legislators who opposed a move to lift a ban on Japanese food imports from the prefectures surrounding the Fukushima nuclear power plant.

The DPP's secessionist claim is getting support in the U.S., with Washington stepping up military and diplomatic support for the island's government. This is part of the new Cold War the U.S. is waging against China.

The U.S. has expanded its naval operations in the South China Sea and Strait of Taiwan. The increasing frequency of the exercises by aircraft carrier strike groups is extremely provocative.

The recent sale of nuclear submarines to Australia as part of the formation of the AUKUS bloc was another aggressive move. AUKUS is an alliance between Australia, Britain and the United States that is clearly aimed at confrontation with China.

The reunification of China after the "century of humiliation" has always been seen as an essential part of building socialist China. The Chinese constitution states: "Taiwan is part of the sacred territory of the People's Republic of China. It is the lofty duty of the entire Chinese people, including our compatriots in Taiwan, to accomplish the great task of reunifying the motherland."

Without warfare or any kind of military incursion, China carried out the reunification of Hong Kong and Macau using an approach called "One Country, Two Systems." Something like this was expected to happen with Taiwan, leading to a gradual reintegration. The Communist Party of China has always stressed its desire to achieve a peaceful reunification with Taiwan.

Sharon Black | August 4, 2022

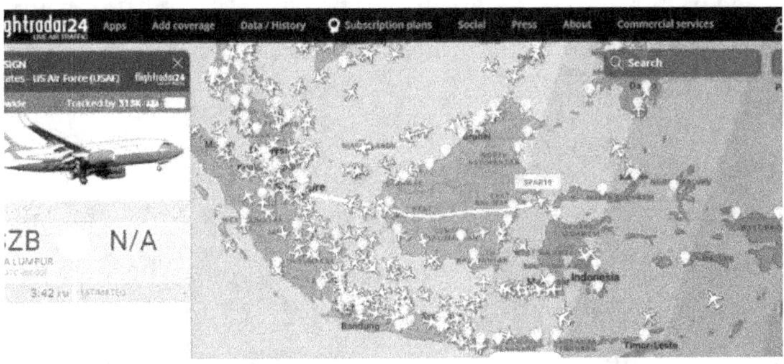

SPAR19 — a U.S. Air Force plane carrying House Speaker Nancy Pelosi from Malaysia to Taiwan as seen on a Flightradar24 map.
Screenshot

No U.S. war on China!

China is no threat to people in the U.S. or the world; Wall Street and Pentagon are

House Speaker Nancy Pelosi, the third highest ranking U.S. government official, landed in Taiwan on August 2. This reckless and aggressive move that infringes on the sovereign rights of over 1.4 billion Chinese people pushes the needle ever closer to a larger, more destructive global war.

The capitalist press portrays Pelosi as a lone individual, a political leader who single-handedly is defying the Chinese government. Nothing can be further from the truth.

Pelosi flew on a U.S. military plane flanked by Air Force F-35 fighters. Instead of flying directly over the South China Sea, her aircraft flew west around the Philippines.

All the while, the massive nuclear-powered USS Ronald Reagan carrier strike group lay nearby. This battle group, armed to the teeth, includes a guided missile cruiser and nuclear submarines.

U.S. violates "One China" policy

Taiwan is part of China, a fact that even the U.S. officially recognizes through the "One China" policy. The U.S. has signed three separate agreements with China confirming the One China policy. "One China" is also recognized by the U.N.

In response to Pelosi's hawkish actions, the Chinese government issued a statement on August 2 that reads, in part:

> "Since the founding of the People's Republic of China in 1949, 181 countries have established diplomatic relations with China on the basis of the one-China principle. The one-China principle is a universal consensus of the international community and a basic norm in international relations.

> "In 1979, the United States made a clear commitment in the China-U.S. Joint Communiqué on the Establishment of Diplomatic Relations — 'The United States of America recognizes the Government of the People's Republic of China as the sole legal Government of China. Within this context, the people of the United States will maintain cultural, commercial, and other unofficial relations with the people of Taiwan.'"

Words and treaties are one thing with U.S. imperialism, but deeds are another. The Indigenous Nations could attest to this.

Pentagon seeks to turn Taiwan into a military outpost

House Speaker Pelosi's visit, while publicly lighting the match, has not been the only action by U.S. imperialism egging on and propping up Taiwan separatism.

In November 2021, Struggle-La Lucha, reported:

"On Oct. 7, (2021) the Wall Street Journal reported that about two dozen U.S. special operations and support troops were 'secretly operating in Taiwan to train military forces there for at least a year.'"

The Global Times points out that:

"Since the U.S. has exposed the news through anonymous officials, it has taken a step forward to undermine, from covertly to semi-overtly, the key conditions for the establishment of diplomatic relations between the Chinese mainland and the U.S."

From the same Struggle-La Lucha report:

"The U.S. government officially recognizes that Taiwan is a province of China, not a separate nation. Therefore, what the Biden administration is now doing — secretly sending special forces into the Chinese province — is in violation of both U.S. and international law."

Additionally, in March 2021, Nikkei Asia reported that the United States was discussing stationing offensive missiles on Taiwan that would have violated the INF treaty.

Taiwan is manufacturing center for semiconductor chips

Taiwan is a major manufacturing center for semiconductor computer chips that power cars, laptops, phones and appliances. It produces 92% of the world's advanced semiconductors.

China is Taiwan's largest trading partner. While China is building semiconductor plants on the mainland, breaking this supply chain is obviously intended to disrupt Chinese global production. The U.S. produces a mere 12%. It faces a shortage because it was more profitable for U.S. businesses to import from Asia.

That's what's behind the Chips and Science Act just passed by Congress on July 28. The act includes more than $52 billion for U.S. companies to take over computer chip production. Reports indicate that the goal is to turn Taiwan production away from China and toward the U.S.

China defends itself

The Chinese People's Liberation Army (PLA) is presently continuing exercises blockading the island. The Global Times reported the details of China's response.

The headline reads: "PLA drills around Taiwan continue to 'rehearse reunification operation' amid Pelosi's visit, 'exercises blockading island to become routine'

"Joint military exercises around the island of Taiwan by the Chinese People's Liberation Army (PLA) continued Wednesday with a joint blockade, sea assault, and land and air combat trainings, involving the use of advanced weapons including J-20 stealth fighter jets and DF-17 hypersonic missiles after the drills started on Tuesday evening when U.S. House Speaker Nancy Pelosi landed on the island which seriously violates China's sovereignty.

"The exercises are unprecedented as the PLA conventional missiles are expected to fly over the island of Taiwan for the first time, the PLA forces will enter the area within 12 nautical miles of the island and the so-called median line will cease to exist, experts said, noting that by surrounding Taiwan entirely, the PLA is completely blockading the island demonstrating the Chinese mainland's absolute control over the Taiwan question."

The U.S./NATO proxy war — the 2014 U.S.-assisted coup and the consequent puppet regime in Ukraine — cannot be ignored by the Communist Party of China. Taiwan as a U.S. colony would be a clear existential threat to Chinese sovereignty.

China cannot allow this, and the Pentagon knows it.

U.S. imperialism wants war – we must organize to stop it!

As the global capitalist crisis deepens, the U.S. imperialist system is propelled toward war. The drive toward war is independent of political administrations or individual intentions, regardless of how venal or corrupt.

The people of the United States have nothing in common with the multi-trillion dollar war industry that profits off of dumping its weapons on Taiwan and all around the globe. The capitalist system and its bankers seek global domination while workers' livelihoods are threatened by inflation and recession.

War brings nothing but more repression, misery, death and climate destruction.

Prepare now: This is not just Pelosi but the whole damn system.

Guided-missile cruisers USS Antietam and USS Chancellorsville share a pier at Naval Station Yokosuk, Japan.

Photo: US Navy

Gary Wilson | Sept.1, 2022

Biden escalates with $1.1 billion arms sale to Taiwan

The Biden administration is set to ramp up its arms sales to Taiwan with numbers that suggest Ukraine levels of escalation.

"The Biden administration plans to formally ask Congress to approve an estimated $1.1 billion arms sale to Taiwan that includes 60 anti-ship missiles and 100 air-to-air missiles, according to three sources with direct knowledge of the package," Politico reports.

According to Politico, the over $1 billion arms package includes "60 AGM-84L Harpoon Block II missiles for $355 million, 100 AIM-9X Block II Sidewinder tactical air-to-air missiles for $85.6 million, and $655.4 million for a surveillance radar contract extension, the people said. The Sidewinder missiles will arm Taipei's U.S.-made F-16 fighter jets."

"When it comes to the Taiwan question, the U.S. president is very much like the general sales manager of a big arms dealer," Global Times writer Hu Xijin commented on Twitter.

The new escalation to send more advanced arms to Taiwan follows a month of four separate U.S. Congressional delegation visits. It started with House Speaker Nancy Pelosi's grandstanding arrival Aug. 2 in a U.S. Air Force Boeing C-40 militarized aircraft.

On Aug. 28, the U.S. Navy sent a pair of warships through the Taiwan Strait for the first time since Pelosi's trip.

U.S. warships in Chinese waters

CNN reported: "The guided-missile cruisers USS Antietam and USS Chancellorsville were on Sunday making the voyage 'through waters where high seas freedoms of navigation and overflight apply in accordance with international law,' the U.S. 7th Fleet in Japan said in a statement."

A spokesperson for the People's Liberation Army's Eastern Theater Command said in response: "Troops of the (Eastern) Theater Command are on high alert and ready to foil any provocation at any time."

"There is no legal basis for 'international waters' in the international law of the sea. It is false to call the Taiwan Strait international waters, Chinese Foreign Ministry spokesman Wang Wenbin said at a regular news conference on June 13 when asked by a reporter from Bloomberg," says Li Huan of the China Institutes of Contemporary International Relations.

Huan adds: "The term 'international waters' used by the Bloomberg reporter is not a formal legal term in the international law of the sea, but it is used informally by some countries to refer to 'high seas.'… Situated between the mainland and the islands of a country, the Taiwan Strait connects the East China Sea and the South China Sea. …

"The Taiwan Strait is approximately 70 nautical miles at its narrowest and about 220 nautical miles at its widest. Under the [1982 United Nations Convention on the Law of the

Sea] and Chinese law, the Taiwan Strait's waters comprise China's internal waters, territorial sea, contiguous zone, and exclusive economic zone. States have different rights and obligations over different waters, and different modes of navigation apply to different waters. …

"U.S. warships this year have been sailing in the Taiwan Strait about once a month on average. … Such [U.S. military] navigation borders on provocation by supporting Taiwan separatists and continually hollowing out and deflating the 'One China' policy.

"In accordance with the convention and Chinese law, China's government enjoys sovereignty and jurisdiction over the waters of the Taiwan Strait, while respecting the legitimate rights of other countries in these waters. If this question is deliberately manipulated using the false claim that China is in violation of the rules of the international law of the sea, China certainly needs" to respond.

The U.S. military already encircles China with a chain of air bases and military ports. It wants to add bases in Taiwan.

Control of computer chip production

"Beyond being a military asset, Taiwan is the global center of production of computer chips, making it crucial for global supply chains and the production of electronics by U.S. companies," Brendan Devlin reports in Passage, an independent media outlet in Canada.

"While in Taiwan, Pelosi had a meeting with the chairman of the Taiwan Semiconductor Manufacturing Corporation. The visit coincides with U.S. efforts to convince the company to set up a manufacturing base in the U.S. and to stop making advanced chips for Chinese companies."

Under the One China policy, the U.S. — like the rest of the world — recognizes Taiwan as a part of China.

The unification of China has always been seen as an essential part of building socialist China.

The Chinese constitution states: "Taiwan is part of the sacred territory of the People's Republic of China. It is the lofty duty of the entire Chinese people, including our compatriots in Taiwan, to accomplish the great task of reunifying the motherland." The Communist Party of China has always stressed its desire to achieve a peaceful reunification with Taiwan.

The escalation of arms from the U.S. to Taiwan, the expanded U.S. naval operations in the South China Sea and Strait of Taiwan, and the increasing frequency of the exercises by aircraft carrier strike groups threaten peace. These are war provocations and must be stopped.

John Parker | Dec. 23, 2022

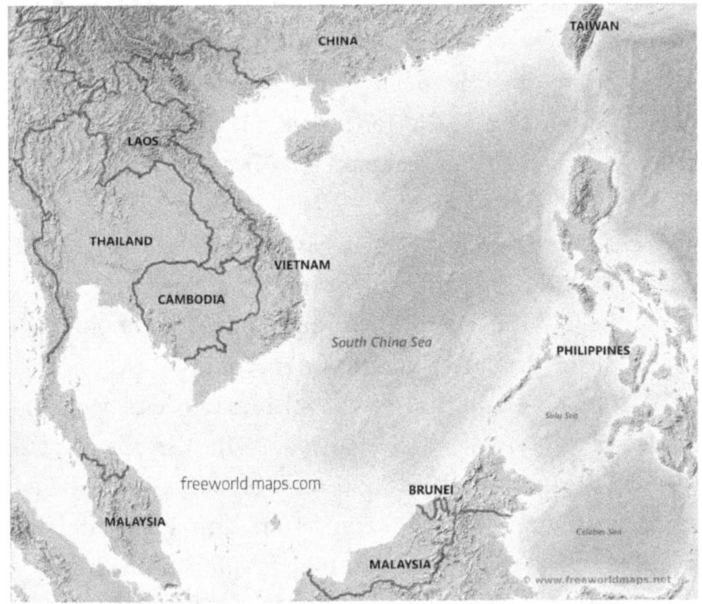

Reckless U.S. war games in South China Sea go against the current

U.S. military exercises have come within 400 miles of China's mainland in the South China Sea (called the South Sea in China and the East Sea in Vietnam). The provocations have increased year after year since former President Obama's imperialist "pivot" towards Asia.

Imagine if China had military exercises right on the doorstep of the U.S. mainland in either the Pacific or Atlantic oceans – close enough for a passenger cruise ship to come into contact with the exercises. And not just your typical military exercises, but ones that were in preparation for a coastal invasion. Imagine if China did this with three other countries, some of whom were promised nuclear weapons.

It's hard to imagine such a scenario targeting the U.S. because it doesn't exist. But for the people of China, the U.S. is very much at the doorstep on a daily basis. And on Nov. 29, the situation escalated.

According to a report in the Nov. 30 China Daily, a U.S. guided-missile cruiser illegally entered Chinese waters near the Nansha Islands on the morning of Nov. 29, a spokesperson from the People's Liberation Army said.

"Without the approval of the Chinese government, the guided-missile cruiser USS Chancellorsville illegally entered the waters near the islands and reefs of China's Nansha Islands on Tuesday," Senior Colonel Tian Junli, spokesman for the PLA Southern Theater Command, said in a statement.

"The theater command has organized naval and air forces to track, monitor and warn it off," he said.

The colonel added that the warship's move, which seriously infringed on China's sovereignty and security, is more "hard proof "that the United States is seeking maritime hegemony and militarizing the South China Sea.

According to the South China Sea Data Initiative, a project of Emory University and the University of California, in 2017, the USS Dewey warship held a "maneuvering drill" less than 400 miles from the mainland of China. In that same year, the USS Stethem came within 200 miles of China's southernmost province, Hainan Island, with a population of about 10 million people.

The U.S. travels over 10,000 miles in the Pacific Ocean to go poking around in the waters of China. Yet if you look

2,000 miles out from the shores of the U.S. on either the Pacific or Atlantic oceans, you see no Chinese military exercises. In fact, you won't find any hostile military exercises anywhere within thousands of miles of U.S. shores.

But Washington arrogantly says China is the guilty party threatening the U.S.

Strategy of provocation

The fact is that, like the strategy to provoke Russia exposed three years ago in the Rand Corporation Plan, this plan to target and provoke China is exposed in the 2022 National Defense Strategy document from the U.S. Secretary of State and blessed by President Joe Biden in its introduction.

The plan was written before this latest provocation in the South China Sea and reveals that these altercations are pre-planned to solicit one result – war with China.

China Daily reported March 29 that a study "by the South China Sea Strategic Situation Probing Initiative, a Beijing-based think-tank tracking U.S. military operations with open source data, said the U.S. carried out at least 95 military exercises in the South China Sea last year, ten more than in 2019."

The article quotes Hu Bo, director of the think-tank, who said the U.S. military has maintained a fairly strong presence near China since 1949, but in recent years it has considerably ramped up its operations in the region and made them more public.

As the National Defense Strategy outlines, these provocations will be carried out with the assistance of other collaborators of U.S. imperialism.

"In August 2021, the U.S., along with Australia, Britain and Japan, carried out 'Large Scale Exercise 21,' its largest naval exercise in 40 years, involving around 25,000 military personnel operating across 17 time zones from Europe to Asia," says China Daily.

Hu warned that Washington's reckless escalation in military activities severely stretched personnel and machinery, leading to a greater risk of accidents and friction in the South China Sea.

For example, the USS Connecticut nuclear submarine recently collided with an uncharted seamount (underwater mountain) in the South China Sea last year, and an F-35C fighter jet crashed on an aircraft carrier operating in the region in January.

"In an era of peace, if one country maintains such a powerful military presence close to another country, it is hard for the former to convince people that it is doing it for peaceful purposes," Hu said.

Driven by profits

What is the U.S. economic interest in the South China Sea?

According to a 2018 CNBC report, the South China Sea has $5.3 trillion worth of trade going through its waters each year, or one-third of all global maritime trade.

It's been estimated that between 11 billion and 125 billion barrels of oil and between 190 trillion and 500 trillion cubic feet of natural gas lies beneath.

But for the U.S., grabbing control has become even more of an uphill battle since it has no NATO forces in the region. Many of the countries it would like to conspire within these provocations toward war have growing beneficial trade relations with China. This includes South Korea.

Moon Chung-in, chairman of the Sejong Institute in the Republic of Korea, quoted by China Daily, mentioned that the U.S. has been implementing its "Indo-Pacific" strategy, a strategy to isolate China economically, but this would hurt South Korea.

"China is our biggest trade partner so we cannot join the U.S. in decoupling with China, but meanwhile, we share similar values with the U.S.," Moon said. "… Thus, we must return to the principles of multilateralism that Beijing has proposed."

China's economic and cultural ties have increased with the Association of Southeast Asian Nations (ASEAN), which was formed to create a more powerful force for maintaining the sovereignty and independence of its member nations. It consists of Brunei Darussalam, Cambodia, Indonesia, Lao People's Democratic Republic, Malaysia, Myanmar, Philippines, Singapore, Thailand, and Vietnam.

According to Shi Zhongjun, secretary-general of the ASEAN-China Centre: "… two-way trade has grown by 85 times from 1991 to 2021, maintaining a robust growth momentum … bilateral trade increased by 15.8% year-on-year in the first ten months of this year to 5.26 trillion yuan ($737.6 billion), accounting for 15.2% of China's foreign trade. And China has become the second-largest investor in ASEAN, with its investment in 2021 touching $14 billion, up 96% year-on-year.

"The two sides have also maintained frequent people-to-people exchanges … with mutual visits exceeding 65 million and the total number of flights between the two sides being more than 4,500 a week in 2019. …

"Chinese universities are offering majors in the official languages of all the ASEAN member states, and the two-way flow of students was more than 200,000 a year before the pandemic broke out."

The reckless strategy laid out in the U.S. National Defense Strategy has little hope of unifying an anti-China conspiracy amongst the ASEAN nations, and without that, the plan will ultimately fail.

What the anti-war movement must do now is hasten that failure. We must build the understanding of who the real provokers of war are instead of allowing the vilification of Russia and China to distract us from stopping all manifestations of U.S. imperialist war strategies.

Gary Wilson | Feb. 7, 2023

Protesters rally outside Philippine military headquarters.

Photo: VCG/Global Times

What's the significance of the 'spy balloon' incident?

While an alleged "spy balloon" dominates the news, U.S. Secretary of Defense Lloyd Austin was just in the Philippines to announce the expansion of U.S. bases in anticipation of war with China over Taiwan.

On Feb. 2, General Austin spoke at a news conference at the Philippine military headquarters in Manila. U.S. troops, ships, and aircraft will be stationed in nine military bases in the Philippines, including a base on the Philippines' most northern island, about 118 miles from Taiwan. This puts the U.S. military in place for a rapid operation in Taiwan.

"This is a big deal," Austin said. "This is a very big deal."

Outside the Philippine military headquarters, dozens of protesters opposed to the U.S. military occupation rallied with chants of "U.S. troops out now" and "Down with U.S. imperialism."

As to the weather balloon, what is significant is not its presence. There have been three or more other times in the last few years that Chinese weather balloons have flown over the U.S., but none of them were reported in the news at the time.

This time the Pentagon announced the balloon's presence "on an espionage mission." The Pentagon managed the daily news reports, not the White House or the State Department. The generals were in charge. It was war propaganda.

All the news coverage in the U.S. called it a spy craft, never a weather research balloon, as China said.

According to a Politico report, Defense Secretary Austin, U.S. Northern Command Chief Gen. Glen VanHerck, and Joint Chiefs Chair Gen. Mark Milley were in charge, giving orders (called "recommendations" in the report) to the White House and the State Department as well as dictating the news reports.

One result was that U.S. Secretary of State Antony Blinken canceled his trip to Beijing for high-level diplomatic talks, which was to be the first secretary of state visit since Michael Pompeo's belligerent confrontation in October 2018.

Blinken's trip had become a focus of war hawks in Congress. Republican senators led by Marco Rubio from Florida signed an open letter to Blinken demanding that the trip be a confrontation with China, particularly focusing on Taiwan.

Signers of the letter, in addition to Rubio, were Senators Chuck Grassley, Bill Cassidy, Eric Schmitt, Dan Sullivan, Kevin Cramer, Ted Budd, Rick Scott, Marsha Blackburn,

Lindsey Graham, Shelley Moore Capito, Pete Ricketts, John Hoeven, and Bill Hagerty.

Not that the Biden administration hasn't followed or even escalated the anti-China policies of the Trump administration. In December, Biden approved $180 million in arms to Taiwan. Biden extended the ban on telecommunications equipment from China's Huawei Technologies and ZTE. And the Biden administration instituted comprehensive restrictions on selling semiconductor chips and manufacturing equipment to China.

Air Force general says war

The Pentagon has been aggressively raising the threat levels.

In a memo dated Feb. 1 but leaked several days earlier, a four-star Air Force general instructed units under his command to begin concrete preparations for war with China that he predicted would come by 2025. Gen. Mike Minihan heads the U.S. Air Mobility Command.

Minihan's memo seems to echo Air Force General Jack Ripper, a character from the 1964 movie "Dr. Strangelove" who orders his command wing to launch a nuclear attack on the Soviet Union.

Minihan lays out a nine-point plan as "preparation for the next fight."

"I hope I am wrong," he commented after the memo was made public. "My gut tells me we will fight in 2025."

Michael McCaul, the new chair of the House Foreign Affairs Committee and the most powerful figure in the House on foreign policy, said on Fox News: "I hope he's wrong as well. I think he's right, though, unfortunately."

That's a war threat.

Japan and Australia

On Jan. 13, Japan's prime minister, Fumio Kishida, met with Biden at the White House, the New York Times reports, "to work together to transform Japan into a potent military power to help counterbalance China and to bolster the alliance between the two nations so that it becomes the linchpin for their security interests in Asia."

Washington and Tokyo are deliberately undermining the basis for diplomatic ties with China — the One China policy recognizing Beijing as the legitimate government of all China, including Taiwan.

"We have to protect Taiwan," Japan's deputy defense minister, Yasuhide Nakayama, said in 2021.

Japan had seized Taiwan in 1895, the beginning of Japan's colonial empire in Asia.

The U.S. has secured military alliances with Japan and the Philippines that makes a north-south arc around Taiwan. A third treaty ally, Australia, is being equipped with nuclear-powered submarines by the U.S. and Britain to operate in the South China Sea. "Attack submarines are a big deal, and they send a big message," the New York Times reported when the fleet of submarines were announced in 2021.

Today, the U.S. is the primary armaments manufacturer and exporter worldwide. Almost 40% of all armaments production in the world is in the U.S. The military industry is the core of manufacturing in the U.S., estimated to be more than 60% of all industrial production and supply in this country.

The military escalation against China was begun by the Trump administration. It should not be forgotten that Donald Trump was, first and foremost, an operative of the military-industrial complex. His cabinet and staff came from Raytheon and Boeing, as well as a slew of U.S. Army officers – generals and colonels. U.S. military expansion increased under Trump.

Trump was the "cheerleader for U.S. arms exports." He touted it as "making America great." The New York Times cheered, too, saying that Trump had revived manufacturing in the U.S.

The weapons industry, of course, directly arms the military for the purpose of expansion and conquest of the world. But arms exports are another way to conquer. A country that adopts U.S. weapons and equipment puts itself under the control of the U.S. systems.

The industrial half of the military-industrial complex drives the arms buildup. It is they who are most in need of expanding the military. The military expansion is the expansion of business.

General Carl Von Clausewitz famously said: "War is the continuation of politics by other means." And politics is concentrated economics, as V.I. Lenin pointed out. The politics producing this war buildup are the economic interests of big business.

Graphic: People's Daily

Scott Scheffer | March 26, 2023

Bipartisan slander of China: Lab leak theory dead, U.S. war drive alive and well

Last week, before the capitalist crisis of bank failures crowded it out of the headlines, news of a congressional hearing to further investigate the origins of the virus that caused the COVID-19 pandemic was splashed across the front pages and websites of major U.S. media.

Trumpists, conspiracy theorists and fascists in the House of Representatives, who now drive the program of the Republican Party, led the charade. It was a means to revive the slanders against China and launch a broadside attack on their Democratic Party rivals, too.

Meanwhile, the China hawks in the Democratic Party and the Biden Administration are content to let them carry the ball. If the lies finally get exposed, the Republican Party will take the heat for the deception. But more important to the China hawks in both parties, the whole affair serves to villainize China and soften anti-war sentiment in preparation for an unthinkable U.S. war.

Even before the House hearings issued their summary report that calls the lab leak lie "most likely," a team of scientists found DNA evidence that shows the virus was spread from bats to other animals and then to humans at the market in Wuhan. Swabs taken from the market soon after the virus began to spread contain DNA of raccoon dogs and DNA of the virus. (Racoon dogs are fox-like animals native to eastern Asia.)

If the House "investigation" had been objective and based on science, the summary report would have been delayed, and the hearing would have taken this evidence into account. The report would have acknowledged that the lab leak theory should be dispensed with and the zoonotic route of the virus is as close to proof as any explanation can be. That didn't happen because the aim of the hearing was simply to damage China's reputation as a world leader in the fight against COVID 19.

The congressional hearing was prompted by a U.S. Department of Energy (DOE) report reasserting the slanders against the lab in Wuhan and claiming a cover-up by China. In spite of no new evidence being included in the report, major U.S. media ran with it, and the House "investigation" followed.

The role of the DOE as supposed investigators of a global health catastrophe shows the falsity of the claims. The DOE gets huge research funds to develop weapons for the Pentagon. Its staff are not virologists, epidemiologists or scientists even remotely connected to health. They monitor and regulate the supply of energy in the U.S. But a lesser known function is that they help the Pentagon by testing, designing, and upgrading the U.S. nuclear weapons stockpile.

Bipartisan slander

In January 2021, a United Nations delegation of scientists and health experts visited China. Their summary report concluded that a lab leak was unlikely and that there should be continued effort to find the route that the virus took – the search for a second mammal that "piggybacked" the virus from bats to humans. But that didn't stop Biden administration officials from continuing to push the China-bashing that escalated during the Trump era and led to a spike in violent anti-Asian attacks.

In May 2021, President Joe Biden sought more anti-China propaganda by ordering spy agencies to investigate. Six agencies did so. Four concluded the virus was likely to have spread from animals. But the FBI and the DOE leaned in the direction of a lab leak. All six reports were issued at a level of "low confidence."

The results must have been somewhat disappointing to Biden, Secretary of State Antony Blinken, and National Security Advisor Jake Sullivan, who were by now the new leaders of the growing anti-China demonization. The lab leak theory was kept alive, though, as China hawks latched onto the missing second mammal that spread COVID-19 from bats to humans. The raccoon dog link was still unknown.

Outside the context of the war drive, where logic and science prevail, the lab leak lie has certainly been dealt a death blow by the discovery of the raccoon dog as the intermediate mammal. In fact, the evidence that COVID-19 was spread naturally from bats to raccoon dogs and then to humans is stronger in a sense than the evidence for zoonotic spread of the virus that caused the SARS outbreak in the early 2000s.

In a March 16 Atlantic article, Gigi Gronvall, a senior scholar at the Johns Hopkins Center for Health Security, said, "I think the evidence is actually more sturdy for COVID than it is for many others.

"The strength of the data might even, in at least one way, best what's available for SARS-CoV-1: Although scientists have isolated SARS-CoV-1-like viruses from a wet-market-traded mammal host, the palm civet, those samples were taken months after the outbreak began — and the viral variants found weren't exactly identical to the ones in human patients.

"The versions of SARS-CoV-2 tugged out of several Huanan-market samples, meanwhile, are a dead ringer for the ones that sickened humans with COVID early on."

Yet there was no outcry for multiple investigations at the time of the SARS outbreak, even though they hadn't confirmed the intermediate mammal that spread it to humans. The Pentagon was then waging its terrible war against the people of Iraq. The new war drive against China and the uptick in Cold War-style fear-mongering had not yet begun. There was no impetus to deny science and spread antagonistic anti-China slanders.

That has changed. Now the U.S. is patrolling near China's territorial waters, using the greater portion of the Pentagon's naval combat forces. That can only spell war. As they try by proxy to destroy Russia, China is also in U.S. imperialism's crosshairs.

We need a global anti-imperialist uprising. Anti-war forces in the U.S. have the potential and the obligation to stop what would be a catastrophic war before it starts.

Gary Wilson | April 28, 2023

Tucker Carlson and the U.S. war on China

Why was Tucker Carlson fired from Fox News? Not for any of his known offensives, even though that's a very long list.

Carlson is the millionaire (net worth $420 million) son of the director of the CIA's Voice of America and Radio Marti directed at Cuba as well as the U.S. Information Agency, whose racist, misogynist, homophobic, anti-immigrant views take 27,407 words to chronicle on Wikipedia. Obviously not a friend of the working class.

Glenn Greenwald, the journalist who started his career as a lawyer for a white supremacist and has been a second banana on Carlson's Fox News show in recent years, suggests that Carlson was fired because "the removal of Tucker means the elimination of the only real, sustained dissent on U.S. militarism." Greenwald claims Carlson "opposed the U.S. proxy war in Ukraine."

If Greenwald was honest, he wouldn't say that Carlson dissented on U.S. militarism; he dissented only on the U.S. proxy war on Russia.

What Carlson says is: "Russia is not America's main enemy ... Our main enemy is China. The U.S. ought to be in a relationship with Russia, aligned against China".

In another broadcast, Carlson said: "The biggest threat to this country is not Vladimir Putin; that's ludicrous. The biggest threat obviously is China."

When Jack Teixeira, the 21-year-old in the Air National Guard's 102nd Intelligence Wing at Otis Airbase, released top-secret Pentagon documents, Rep. Marjorie Taylor Greene praised him as "white, male, christian, and antiwar ... he told the truth about [U.S.] troops being on the ground in Ukraine and a lot more."

Really? This guy, who was known for his racist and anti-Semitic postings, was never antiwar, though he may have opposed the U.S. proxy war on Russia. That's what Tucker Carlson said, that Teixeira's leaks "prove U.S. troops are fighting in Ukraine."

Actually, that part is true. The U.S. and NATO started training Ukrainian forces to fight in Donbass in 2015, and while the training is now done in other countries, NATO provides six-month training courses to all of Ukraine's forces.

The leaked Pentagon documents revealed that in addition to military trainers and "consultants" in Ukraine, the U.S. has about a hundred special forces personnel operating there, including 14 who are part of a special forces unit made up mostly of "elite" British SAS soldiers.

The leaked Pentagon documents also show a buildup in Pentagon operations targeting China, including assessments that could be used for a U.S. military intervention in Taiwan.

Divisions in U.S. ruling class

The documents also reveal what the Washington Post calls "the U.S.'s gloominess on the war in Ukraine."

"The [Washington Post] admits that Western media audiences have been misled about the course of the war, that essentially what mainstream media has been reporting about Ukraine has been a pack of lies: namely that Ukraine is winning the war and is poised to launch an offensive that will lead to a final victory," reports Joe Lauria in Consortium News.

"Instead, the second paragraph of the piece makes clear the leaked documents show the long-planned Ukrainian offensive will fail miserably — 'a marked departure from the Biden administration's public statements about the vitality of Ukraine's military,' Lauria continues.

"In other words, U.S. officials have been lying about the state of the war to the public and to reporters who have faithfully reported their every word without a hint of skepticism," he concludes.

The documents show there are sections of the U.S. ruling class who are worried about the disastrous proxy war in Ukraine. The death toll has been rising steadily, and the economic costs of the war are mounting.

The war is also having a destabilizing effect on the global economy, with the price of oil and gas rising sharply and inflation spiraling in the U.S. and Europe. It could disrupt the U.S. war buildup against China.

That's the fear being voiced by Tucker Carlson, Glenn Greenwald, Representative Greene, the Pentagon leaker, and their kind.

The U.S. war on China is dominant in Washington now. As Financial Times columnist Gideon Rachman noted on April 24: "Visiting Washington last week, it was striking how commonplace talk of war between the U.S. and China has become. That discussion has been fed by loose-lipped statements from American generals musing about potential dates for the opening of hostilities. …

"They are a reflection of the broader discussion on China taking place in Washington — inside and outside government. Many influential people seem to think that a U.S.-China war is not only possible but probable."

Gary Wilson | May 2, 2023

The U.S. is docking nuclear-armed submarines in South Korea for the first time since the 1980s.

Photo: U.S. Navy

Biden nukes Korea, builds anti-China alliances

On April 26, in the 'Washington Declaration,' the Biden administration announced that the U.S. would be docking nuclear-armed submarines in South Korea for the first time since the 1980s. The U.S. had withdrawn its open nuclear weapons from South Korea in 1992 with the "Joint Declaration of South and North Korea on the Denuclearization of the Korean Peninsula" treaty.

Although it was widely believed that the U.S. continued to secretly deploy nuclear weapons in Korea, this move by the Biden administration is a blatant violation of the denuclearization treaty.

The deployment of nuclear-armed submarines is an escalation bringing the Korean peninsula to the "brink of a nuclear war," the Korean Central News Agency reported on May 1.

"So far, the U.S. has staged large-scale combined military exercises and all sorts of war drills against the DPRK [Democratic People's Republic of Korea]," the Pyongyang daily Rodong Sinmun reported on May 1, referring to the mass flight of U.S. Air Force nuclear-capable B52 bombers over the Korean peninsula on April 5. Now, the U.S. is "deploying strategic nuclear bombers, nuclear carrier task forces and even strategic nuclear submarines near the territorial waters of the DPRK and makes it public."

The U.S. has not attempted to conceal that the exercises were intended to simulate an attack on the DPRK.

Rodong Sinmun continues, "What is more serious is that U.S. President Biden dared to make frantic and reckless remarks about 'the end of regime' [of] the DPRK while becoming vociferous about a 'swift, overwhelming and decisive response' at a press conference after the talks."

North Korean leader Kim Yo Jong said Biden's threat should not be dismissed as simply a "nonsensical remark from the person in his dotage."

She said, "When we consider that this expression was personally used by the president of the U.S., our most hostile adversary, it is threatening rhetoric for which he should be prepared for far too great an after-storm."

The more the U.S. is "dead set on staging nuclear war exercises, and the more nuclear assets they deploy in the vicinity of the Korean peninsula, the stronger the exercise of our right to self-defense will become in direct proportion to them."

Third-largest U.S. military occupation

According to data from the Pentagon, about 30,000 U.S. troops are stationed in South Korea, the third-largest military presence outside the country after Japan and Germany. In addition, U.S. Forces Korea (USFK) operates about 90 combat planes, 40 attack helicopters, 50 tanks, and some 60 Patriot missile launchers.

The "Washington Declaration" was part of a summit between President Biden and South Korea's far-right President Yoon Suk Yeol.

"According to the New England Korea Peace Campaign, Boston Candlelight Action Committee, and Massachusetts Peace Action, which are preparing to hold a protest on Friday, April 28, in Cambridge, Massachusetts, during Yoon's visit to Harvard, 'Since entering office, Yoon's right-wing administration has expanded costly and provocative U.S.-ROK military exercises, heightened tensions with North Korea, rolled back workers' rights, threatened to abolish the ministry of gender equality, and has taken many other actions to undermine struggles for peace and justice in South Korea,'" Simone Chun reports.

"Yoon's state visit comes at a time when South Korea is experiencing unprecedented crises on the political, economic, and national security fronts as a consequence of the Biden administration's unrelenting pressure on South Korea to join the U.S. anti-China bloc," Chun adds.

The joint statement issued by Biden and Yoon Suk Yeol did not explicitly mention China, but it did make several references to the "free and open Indo-Pacific," which is seen by many as a code phrase for "containing" China.

The statement also declared, "The Presidents reiterated the importance of preserving peace and stability in the Taiwan Strait as an indispensable element of security and prosperity in the region."

Ending 'One China' policy

The U.S. is now targeting Taiwan, virtually ending the "One China" policy that recognizes that Taiwan is part of China. In recent years, the U.S. has increased arms sales to Taiwan, sent high-level officials and Congressional delegations, and conducted joint military exercises with Taiwan. In addition, the U.S. has quadrupled the number of U.S. troops on the island.

Washington is building a system of alliances throughout the Indo-Pacific as part of its war buildup against China. These alliances include the Quadrilateral Security Dialogue (Quad) — Australia, India, Japan, and the U.S. — and the AUKUS pact made up of Australia, Britain, and the U.S.

On April 11, Al Jazeera reported that the U.S. and the Philippines began their largest-ever military drills, including a live-fire exercise on a ship in the South China Sea.

The drills, known as Balikatan, have about 12,200 U.S. troops, 5,400 Armed Forces of the Philippines (AFP) members, and representatives from other countries, including Australia. Balikatan means "shoulder to shoulder" in Tagalog.

The Philippines recently agreed to allow the U.S. access to more military bases under the Enhanced Defense Cooperation Agreement (EDCA). Nine EDCA bases are planned, with four directly facing Taiwan. The Philippines is also increasing military ties with Japan.

Biden has persisted in his aggressive rhetoric on Taiwan. He told CBS News last September that he would send U.S. troops to "defend" Taiwan. Then, in a significant break with the longstanding U.S. "One China" policy, he added: "Taiwan makes their own judgments about their independence… That's their decision."

Of course, Taiwan is part of China and not "independent." Any U.S. military invasion to "defend" Taiwan would be an act of war against China.

China not an imperialist power

As Foreign Policy magazine noted recently, "China is not a superpower." The report uses the term superpower to avoid the more direct and accurate phrase imperialist power, which the U.S. tries to deny.

"The United States is undoubtedly a superpower, with a worldwide network of alliance agreements and overseas bases enabling it to deploy and move forces rapidly between various theaters," FP reports. "China, however, is only a regional power. It wields global economic power and influence, but the geographic reach of its military is largely limited to the Asian and Indo-Pacific theaters."

The United States has direct and unhindered access to the Atlantic, Pacific, and Arctic oceans. China has limited access to the Pacific and is mostly hemmed in by major island chains it does not control.

Imperialist "gunboat diplomacy" requires boats, and airplanes need airfields to operate in far-flung regions. China has none of them, either.

China has only one overseas base — its naval facility in Djibouti, staffed with 400 Chinese marines.

While the U.S. Navy plows the world's oceans daily, the Chinese navy conducts missions only in its own Indo-Pacific area.

A superpower means military and economic dominance over other countries, which China has never had. The U.S., in contrast, has hegemonic dominance over countries in every continent because no other state is in a position to challenge its dominance, FP concludes.

Scott Scheffer | May 20, 2023

U.S. Army rocket system used for a live fire event during Balikatan 23 war exercises in the Philippines, April 26.
Credit U.S. Marine Corps

Biden drops 'One China' policy, uses Philippines for war drive over Taiwan

Pentagon strategists have been beefing up their military presence in Asia and building alliances in preparation for an all-out war against China. In recent months Taiwan has increasingly come into focus as the likely excuse to justify a war as terrible – or worse — than any in modern history.

They want to use Taiwan as a tool to "manufacture consent." But the island is important for more than just war propaganda. Pentagon planners are readying plans for control of areas of Asia and, in particular, the South China Sea that would be of value in war.

In early April, CNN reported that U.S. forces would now be allowed to rotate troops to nine military bases in the Philippines, including four new bases. Three of the four are within a few hundred miles of Taiwan and close to military defense locations of China's People's Liberation Army.

The Philippines bases would facilitate a takeover of the channel between northern Luzon and Taiwan – the area called the Bashi Channel. Control of Taiwan would be instrumental in moving into the South China Sea.

Only weeks after securing access to the bases, the U.S. conducted war exercises jointly with the Armed Forces of the Philippines (AFP). Annual Balikatan war exercises between the U.S. and the Philippines have been growing in size and scope in their decades-long history, and this was the largest ever, involving 17,600 troops – nearly double that in 2022.

More than 12,000 of the troops were from the U.S., a small number from Australia, and the remainder from the AFP. They used live ammunition, F-16 fighter jets, the F-35B stealth bomber, Patriot missile batteries, and Blackhawk and Chinook helicopters. They included amphibious landing practice, and targeted and sunk a decommissioned ship close to the South China Sea.

Balikatan 2023 was an open threat and practice for war against China.

In another signal of the heightened war danger, Philippines President Ferdinand Marcos Jr. followed up with an announcement that the AFP would join the U.S. in ongoing naval patrols of the South China Sea. Marcos' father was a brutal U.S.-backed dictator who was driven into exile by an uprising of the Filipino people in 1986.

War budget, arms sales

On March 9, Secretary of Defense Lloyd Austin announced President Joe Biden's proposed Fiscal Year 2024 Defense Budget of $842 billion – which is $26 billion more than 2023.

Describing Biden's proposal, Austin said: "To sustain our military advantage over China, it makes major investments in integrated air and missile defenses and operational energy efficiency, as well as in our air dominance, our maritime dominance, and in munitions, including hypersonics.

"This budget includes the largest ever request for the Pacific Deterrence Initiative, which we are using to invest in advanced capabilities, new operational concepts, and more resilient force posture in the Indo-Pacific region. It also enables groundbreaking posture initiatives in Guam, Mariana Islands, the Philippines, Japan, and Australia."

Separate from the proposed defense budget, the Biden administration has approved $19 billion in arm sales to Taiwan. Weapons makers are energetically pushing for more of that.

Defense News reported May 3, "A delegation of United States defense contractors and a former senior leader of the U.S. Marine Corps pledged the beginning of deeper cooperation with Taiwan.

"Speaking at a public forum in Taiwan's capital Taipei, retired Lt. Gen. Steven Rudder said the U.S. wants to be part of the defense capabilities of Taiwan and improve the supply chain resilience of the island. He also emphasized how critical the island's position is for security."

Taiwan was already part of China more than a century before George Washington was elected the first president of the U.S. Its unwarranted recognition as a separate country only happened in 1949 when Chiang Kai-Shek, the nationalist leader who slaughtered hundreds of thousands of Mao Zedong's revolutionary fighters beginning with the 1927 Shanghai Massacre, was finally chased out.

Chiang fled to Taiwan and was recognized by the imperialist powers of the U.S. and Britain as the legitimate government of China. Under pressure from the U.S., the United Nations didn't even grant the People's Republic of China a seat until 1971.

Since then, officially, the U.S. has adhered to the "One China" policy in recognition of the fact that Taiwan is part of China. The "Three Communiques" were mutually agreed on policies that the U.S. ostensibly accepted in exchange for the right to invest in China.

Two trends of thought have competed with each other among those billionaires who dominate U.S. policy toward China. There are those who want to maintain a stable profit-taking relationship.

But the spectacular successes of China in lifting more than 800 million people out of extreme poverty, China's rise as a world scientific power, its global leadership in surviving the COVID-19 pandemic, and myriad other achievements have emboldened those capitalist rulers who want to destroy China.

The anti-imperialist movement is facing its greatest challenge in many decades. The proxy war against Russia and the growing momentum for war against China have to be seen as one. A powerful people's movement that takes militant action against U.S. imperialism can and must block another calamitous war.

Gary Wilson | July 3, 2023

U.S. F-22s and the balloon.

Photos: Master Sgt. Kevin J. Gruenwald of F-22s /
LiveStormChasers.com of balloon

Not a spy balloon,
but the propaganda sticks

On Feb. 4, the U.S. Air Force carried out an elaborate operation to shoot down a Chinese weather balloon.

At 2:39 p.m. Eastern time, an F-22 Raptor from the 1st Fighter Wing at Joint Base Langley-Eustis, Virginia, fired an AIM-9X Sidewinder into the approximately 90-foot-wide balloon, causing it to fall towards the Atlantic Ocean, according to U.S. military officials.

At the time, war tensions were rising. The Pentagon managed the daily news reports. The generals were in charge.

But it was all propaganda. All the news coverage in the U.S. called it a spy craft, never a weather research balloon, as China said.

Nothing the Pentagon and White House said at the time was true, and they knew it. But the purpose wasn't to speak truth; the purpose was to justify the Pentagon's war buildup against China.

Now, the Pentagon admits that the balloon was not a spy balloon. Reuters reported on June 29 that the Pentagon now says that the Chinese balloon wasn't a spy craft and it did not collect any information while in U.S. airspace. This is exactly opposite from what they said back in February, claiming it was a spy balloon that had collected intelligence on U.S. military sites.

The Pentagon says that after a reassessment based on an analysis of the balloon's components and flight path, the balloon did not have the necessary equipment to collect intelligence and was not flying in a pattern that would have allowed it to do so.

Also, President Biden acknowledged that the balloon had been blown off course. He said the U.S. government knows the balloon was originally intended to fly over the Pacific Ocean but had been caught in a strong wind current that carried it over land. Biden also said that China had no intention of letting the balloon cross Canada and the United States.

Of course, this news hasn't made it to any front pages or top stories in the big business media. That's because the war propaganda against China isn't over.

Gary Wilson | July 26, 2023

Treasury Secretary Janet Yellen seemed openly insincere when she tried to say the controls were not aimed at China's broader economy. Premier Li Qiang, who met Yellen, responded that she was "overstretching."

The U.S. 'Act of War' against China

The July 12 New York Times Magazine headlined: "'An Act of War': Inside America's Silicon Blockade Against China."

The report is about the October 2022 "export controls" against China:

"Last October, the United States Bureau of Industry and Security issued a document that — underneath its 139 pages of dense bureaucratic jargon and minute technical detail — amounted to a declaration of economic war on China. ...

"The Oct. 7 controls essentially seek to eradicate, root and branch, China's entire ecosystem of advanced technology. 'The new policy embodied in Oct. 7 is: Not only are we not going to allow China to progress any further technological-ly, we are going to actively reverse their current state of the art,' [Gregory] Allen [of the Center for Strategic and International Studies in Washington] says. C.J. Muse, a senior semiconductor analyst at Evercore ISI, put it this way: 'If you'd told me about these rules five years ago, I would've told you that's an act of war — we'd have to be at war.'"

The U.S. export controls (the act of war) on computer chips aim to undermine China's ability to produce or purchase high-end chips, which are crucial for the development of advanced technologies such as supercomputers and artificial intelligence (AI). Some call this a Silicon Curtain in the New Cold War against China.

The U.S. controls (again, an act of war) are not narrowly targeted at curbing Chinese military development, as claimed by the Biden administration. On her recent visit to China, Treasury Secretary Janet Yellen seemed openly insincere when she tried to say the controls were not aimed at the broader economy. China's Premier Li Qiang, who met Yellen, told her that she was "overstretching."

The export controls are broad. As the New York Times reports, they seek to undermine China's entire ecosystem of advanced technology, including its AI industry. The semiconductor industry is seen as a means to achieve this goal.

The semiconductor industry is a global industry that the U.S. has dominated and controlled, as U.S. Big Oil has dominated the global energy industry.

The Pentagon's semiconductor project

The semiconductor industry began as a project of the Pentagon's Semiconductor Technology Advanced Research Network (STARnet), part of the Defense Advanced Research Projects Agency (DARPA). The industry in the U.S. was and is, to this day, heavily financed by the Pentagon and the U.S. government.

The CHIPS Act, passed by Congress and signed by President Biden in August 2022, pumped an additional $280 billion in new funding for the research and manufacture of semiconductors in the U.S. That was followed by a DARPA announcement in January 2023 that it was putting almost half a billion dollars into a project to help advance the semiconductor industry in the U.S.

None of this, by the way, was created or developed by any capitalist entrepreneur. Capitalism does not create anything on its own; it just finds a way to exploit new technology to make a profit. And many of the biggest, highest profit-making capitalist industries were created and funded by the government in various ways, including most of the technology industry, the internet, the pharmaceutical industry, the automobile industry, and even Big Oil.

The semiconductor industry is a knowledge-intensive industry. It is built on shared knowledge and resources. Initially, semiconductor companies were built on open innovation. Because of its complexity, development, and production required the collaboration of research centers, universities, scientists, engineers, and many others to develop the techniques and methodologies required.

The pace of innovation in the semiconductor industry has been incredibly rapid. New chip designs are constantly being developed, and the capabilities of chips are constantly increasing. This is due to a number of factors, including:

- The increasing complexity of chips. Chips are becoming increasingly complex, with billions of transistors packed into a tiny space. This complexity requires the use of advanced manufacturing techniques and the development of new materials.

- New materials and manufacturing techniques. The semiconductor industry is constantly developing new materials and manufacturing techniques to improve the performance and efficiency of chips. For example, new materials, such as gallium arsenide, silicon carbide, and graphene, have allowed for the development of faster and more powerful chips.

- The increasing availability of computing power. The increasing availability of computing power has allowed chip designers to develop more complex and sophisticated chip designs.

Global means global

Global means that chips are designed and manufactured in many countries around the world, not just the U.S. This means:

- A global workforce of scientists, engineers, technicians, and other skilled workers. The semiconductor industry requires a large pool of skilled labor. This labor is not evenly distributed around the world. Most of the semiconductor industry is now concentrated in China, Taiwan, and South Korea.

- As a global industry, production depends on a complicated matrix of manufacturing, warehousing, shipping, and transportation. This global supply chain is highly interconnected and spans across many countries. Every chip has been produced from parts developed and produced in a dozen or more countries. This necessitates collaboration and sharing to ensure smooth operations and product quality.

The U.S. export restrictions (an act of war) are designed not only to prevent further advances in China's technology sector but also to actively reverse its technological development. The controls are intended to eradicate China's advanced technology ecosystem and hinder its progress in economic growth and development.

U.S. export controls, introduced by the Trump administration and now expanded by the Biden administration, have already had devastating consequences for Chinese companies like Huawei, which was heavily impacted by the chip bans imposed by the Trump administration in 2019. Huawei, once the largest smartphone seller in the world, saw its revenues plunge and its market share drastically decline as a result of these measures.

Biden expands what Trump started

The Biden administration has continued the Trump administration's campaign against Chinese technology companies, but it has taken a more expanded approach. The Trump administration imposed broad sanctions on Chinese companies, including Huawei, ZTE, and Hikvision. The Biden administration has focused on whole industries, such as telecommunications and semiconductors.

In the words of Gregory Allen at CSIS, "The Trump administration went after companies. The Biden administration is going after industries."

The Biden administration's actions against China's technology sector are an attempt to slow down the entire Chinese economy. China is heavily reliant on semiconductors, and the Biden administration's actions are making it more difficult for China to acquire the technology and components it needs to produce its own chips.

The fact that China spent more on computer chip imports than it did on oil in April is a clear indication of how important semiconductors are to the Chinese economy. Chips are used in a wide range of products, from smartphones to cars to industrial machinery.

But the New Cold War and its Silicon Curtain cannot reproduce the old Cold War.

In the Cold War, the United States and the European imperialist powers in NATO were the biggest manufacturers in the world. This gave them dominance in terms of economic power and military strength.

Now, socialist China has emerged as a major manufacturing power. Today, China is the world's largest manufacturer, including the semiconductor industry. China is the largest trade partner for 70% of the countries in the world.

This has led to a decline in the United States' relative power. The United States is no longer the dominant producer in the world.

In addition, the U.S. used to have a significant advantage in the global energy market, due to its control of West Asia's hydrocarbon resources. However, in recent years, China has become a major player in the global energy market, and OPEC has become less reliant on the United States. The U.S. has greatly reduced oil imports because of domestic shale oil (fracking) and gas production. This means that OPEC is no longer as dependent on the United States as it once was. This has led to a loss of control for the United States in the global energy market.

Gary Wilson | August 2, 2023

July 30 protest outside the Enoggera Army Base in Australia as the U.S. and Australia engaged in the massive Talisman Sabre anti-China war games.

Photo: Alex Bainbridge

Biden sends $345 million in weapons to Taiwan: Activists protest U.S.-Australia anti-China war games

The Biden administration announced a $345 million weapons package for Taiwan on July 28. The package includes a variety of weapons systems, including Reaper drones, Harpoon anti-ship missiles, Stinger anti-aircraft missiles, and TOW anti-tank missiles.

This is the first part of a $1 billion weapons transfer directly from Pentagon stockpiles to Taiwan this year.

The transfer of weapons from the U.S. to Taiwan is a violation of Chinese sovereignty under international law, which recognizes Taiwan as an island province of China.

The United States does not officially recognize Taiwan as an independent country.

The MQ-9A Reaper is a long-endurance, medium-altitude, unmanned aerial vehicle (UAV) that is used for surveillance and strike missions. It is equipped with a variety of sensors, including a radar, a camera, and a laser designator. The Reaper can also carry a variety of weapons, including Hellfire missiles and laser-guided bombs.

The drones will be used to gather intelligence and could be used to strike population centers in mainland China, as Ukraine is doing with drone strikes on civilian apartment buildings in Moscow.

The transfer of the MQ-9A Reapers to Taiwan is a significant development, as it is the first time that the U.S. has sent this type of drone to a country in the Asia-Pacific region. It is clearly a significant increase in the U.S. military threat against China.

Politico reported: "The package marks the first time the U.S. has used new authority from Congress to transfer military equipment directly from Pentagon inventory to Taiwan. The transfer is done under the Presidential Drawdown Authority, the same mechanism Washington uses to send weapons to Ukraine."

On July 21, the U.S. and Australia began two weeks of "Talisman Sabre war games" involving more than 30,000 troops and participants from 11 other countries, in a show of force against China, Reuters reported.

"This year will see Germany participate for the first time, with 210 paratroopers and marines taking part as the European nation bolsters its presence in the Indo-Pacific," Reuters adds.

Shinako Oyakama
speaking.

Photo: Alex Bainbridge

Nim Flores from
Guayan (Guam).

Photo: Alex Bainbridge

Activists from around Australia joined guests from the
Pacific to speak out against the Talisman Sabre war training on July 30 outside the Enoggera Army Base, Green Left
reported. The protest heard from guests who addressed
the "Calling for Peace in the Pacific" conference, including
Indigenous women Naek Flores from Guahan (Guam) and
Shinako Oyakama from Ryukyu (Okinawa).

U.S. military bases surrounding China, from John Pilger's
The Coming War With China.

Source: Consortium News

Brian Berletic | September 9, 2023

Washington's expanding military footprint on China's doorsteps

A series of announcements by the U.S. reflects its large and still growing military presence across Asia-Pacific, particularly in East and Southeast Asia. Together, they reflect a continued and increasingly desperate desire by Washington to encircle and contain China.

These announcements include plans for expanding the number of U.S. air bases across the region as part of the U.S. Air Force's (USAF) new "Agile Combat Employment" (ACE) doctrine. It also includes plans for a "civilian port" in the Batanes islands, less than 200 km from the Chinese island province of Taiwan. Then there were recently announced plans by the U.S. Department of Defense to create drone swarms for countering China's growing advantage in materiel and manpower.

Washington's "ACE" in the Hole?

A recent article published by Defense One titled "Air Force expanding number of bases in Pacific over next decade," reported on the Pentagon's plans to expand the number of air bases across the Pacific over the next decade to fulfill the requirements of the U.S.AF's "ACE" doctrine.

More than simply increasing the number of air bases in the region, ACE seeks to disperse U.S. aircraft, ammunition, and personnel among a larger number of smaller bases, thus creating more targets for potential adversaries and increasing the overall survivability for U.S.AF assets.

The article notes:

> The U.S. Air Force will increase its number of bases across the Pacific over the next decade, in an effort to spread out and become more survivable in conflict.

And that:

> In the ACE concept, a few airfields serve as central ports, or hubs, while several smaller airfields serve as spokes. The idea is to be able to distribute weapons and assets over a large area and to increase survivability, versus just having a few large airfields throughout the geographically enormous region.

Despite U.S.AF assets being distributed, command and control would be able to mass together assets from across multiple smaller bases for each specific mission or "force package."

The concept is meant to make it more difficult in a potential conflict with China for it to target and destroy U.S. air bases with its large missile arsenals and, by doing so, significantly disrupting U.S. air capabilities in the region.

While ACE doctrine may be a realistic shift away from the relatively centralized nature of U.S. military bases across the Pacific, it will take many years to implement and only if the Pentagon's budget is adjusted to do so. By then, China's missile arsenal will only have increased in size and capabilities, possibly neutralizing any advantage the U.S. seeks to achieve by pursuing this doctrinal shift.

And while an eventual dispersal of U.S. air assets may complicate China's ability to target and destroy U.S. warplanes before even leaving the ground to perform missions, China also possesses a large and very capable integrated air defense system able to intercept both U.S. warplanes and the munitions they would be using against Chinese targets.

U.S. seeks 'civilian port' dangerously close to Taiwan

Reuters, in an article titled "Exclusive: U.S. military in talks to develop port in Philippines facing Taiwan," would report:

The U.S. military is in talks to develop a civilian port in the remote northernmost islands of the Philippines, the local governor and two other officials told Reuters, a move that would boost American access to strategically located islands facing Taiwan.

U.S. military involvement in the proposed port in the Batanes islands, less than 200 km (125 miles) from Taiwan, could stoke tensions at a time of growing friction with China and a drive by Washington to intensify its longstanding defence treaty engagement with the Philippines.

The article also notes:

The Bashi Channel between those islands and Taiwan is considered a choke point for vessels moving between the western Pacific and the contested South China Sea and a key waterway in the case of a Chinese invasion of Taiwan. The Chinese military regularly sends ships and aircraft through the channel, Taiwan's defence ministry has said.

The article fails to mention a much more important fact, that this "choke point" leading into the "contested South China Sea" is already "a key waterway," one for Chinese maritime shipping.

While the U.S. poses as underwriting peace, stability, and prosperity in the "Indo-Pacific" region and, more specifically, in upholding "freedom of navigation" in areas like the South China Sea, the reality is that most of the "navigation" taking place in these waters is trade moving to and from China between other nations in the region which consider China their largest trade partner.

U.S. government and arms industry-funded think tank, the Center for Strategic and International Studies (CSIS), as part of its "China Power" project, published a post titled, "How Much Trade Transits the South China Sea?" It included an interactive map indicating the percentage of trade that flowed through the South China Sea from each nation.

China, by far, was the largest beneficiary of navigation through the South China Sea, accounting for over a quarter of all trade passing through it. South Korea (7%), Japan (4%), and Southeast Asian nations like Thailand (5%), Vietnam (5%), and Singapore (6%) also accounted for large percentages of trade through the sea, with each of these nations counting China as their largest trade partner.

Very clearly, the U.S., by expanding its military presence in and around the South China Sea, including at choke points like the Batanes islands, is best positioned to threaten, not protect, maritime shipping in the region, which would hurt China first and foremost. But it would also hurt trade among Washington's supposed "allies" in the region it seeks to recruit in its escalating confrontation with Beijing.

Within the pages of U.S. government-funded think tank documents detailing war games between the U.S. and China, the disruption of Chinese commerce is a key element of

Washington's strategy. By creating a "civilian port" at the northernmost reach of the Philippines, so close to Taiwan and at a critical choke point leading in and out of the South China Sea, the U.S. is placing itself one step closer to a better position from which to launch a war against China.

Drone swarms aimed at China

Defense One, in another article titled "'Hellscape': DOD launches massive drone swarm program to counter China," would report:

China's most important asset in potential war with the United States is "mass," says Deputy Defense Secretary Kathleen Hicks: "More ships. More missiles. More people."

To counter that advantage, the Defense Department will launch an initiative called Replicator to create cheap drones across the air, sea, and land in the "multiple thousands" within the next two years.

Cheap drones, of the type Ukraine has deployed to great effect against Russia, can be produced close to the battlefield at much lower cost than typical Defense Department weapons.

While at first glance, the strategy may seem sound, within the article itself, the primary problem with these plans reveals itself. The proliferation of swarms of cheap drones being used by both sides in Ukraine is made possible by easy-to-purchase Chinese-made components.

The whole reason China has "more ships" and "more missiles" than the United States in the first place is because of its much larger industrial base. Whatever drone swarm the U.S. may be preparing for China, China will have the capacity to create one much larger to strike back with.

A future war with China

Amid the current conflict in Ukraine, Ukrainian drones have repeatedly targeted Russian air bases deep within Russian territory. Despite the vast majority of these drones being disabled or intercepted, small numbers still occasionally make it through, causing damage. Had Ukraine possessed greater long-range strike capabilities or were Russian air defenses less capable, the damage to these centralized air bases could have been much greater and may have even potentially disrupted Russian combat operations.

The wisdom behind the U.S. Air Force's "ACE" doctrine is apparent. Should Russia adopt a similar doctrine, distributing its warplanes over a larger number of smaller airfields, the rare instances of success Ukraine currently achieves would be even rarer still.

China is certainly learning from the ongoing conflict in Ukraine and is likely studying the posture of its own air assets in relation to the U.S. military's build-up and plans to not only disperse their assets over a wider number of smaller facilities but also their plans to utilize drone swarms in addition to other long-range strike capabilities on a scale much larger than Ukraine is currently using.

Finally, as the U.S. moves closer and closer to Chinese territory with its military and "civilian" infrastructure, and specifically near "choke points" that could potentially restrict or cut off Chinese maritime shipping, Beijing must consider contingencies to sustain its economy including its trade even under the worst-case scenario.

In many ways, the "Belt and Road Initiative" (BRI) already partially accomplishes this. Growing trade with Russia across Russia and China's shared border represents another means of maintaining essential trade, including the flow of energy and raw materials, even if the U.S. implements a naval blockade in the Indo-Pacific.

Taken together, it is clear the U.S. is moving as quickly as possible to position itself best for a coming conflict with China. While U.S. leaders and the Western media suggest China is rushing to war "by 2025," it is clear that time is on China's side and that it is the U.S. rushing to war.

The economic and industrial advantages China enjoys over the U.S. today did not exist 2–3 decades ago. A decade from now, however, China's advantages over the U.S. industrially and thus militarily will only have grown. The U.S. seeks to exploit a closing window of opportunity to fight now before the odds tilt any further in China's favor. But considering the realities of these recent announcements by the U.S. and how little they actually change the odds in Washington's favor, some may conclude that the window has already shut.

Brian Berletic is a Bangkok-based geopolitical researcher and writer, especially for the online magazine "New Eastern Outlook."

The Maritime Self-Defense Force ship JS Kurama leads a formation with U.S. guided missile destroyers during a war exercise. The Japanese Self-Defense Force flys the imperial "rising sun" flag rather than the Japanese national flag which is only the red sun on a white field. The rising sun flag is associated with Japanese militarism and imperialism and is seen to be directed particularly at North Korea and China.

Gary Wilson | January 3, 2023

Japan rearms at U.S. urging: Targets China, North Korea, Russia

The radical new defense strategy announced on Dec. 16 by Japan's Prime Minister Fumio Kishida doubles military spending — a five-year, $320-billion military buildup to secure offensive strike capacity, which is forbidden in Japan's 1947 U.S.-created constitution.

The constitution says that Japan renounces war as a sovereign right and declares that "land, sea and air forces, as well as other war potential, will never be maintained."

The new defense strategy, intended to counter this constitutional provision directly, was initiated at the urging of Washington. The U.S. is actively militarizing the Pacific region – especially Japan – to target China.

The New York Times praised Japan's remilitarization, saying it met the need for a "more muscular military" aimed at China.

The U.S. ambassador to Japan, Rahm Emanuel, said in a statement that "the Prime Minister is making a clear, unambiguous strategic statement about Japan's role as a security provider in the Indo-Pacific."

U.S. Secretary of Defense Lloyd Austin said, "We welcome the release of Japan's updated strategy documents …

which reflect Japan's staunch commitment to upholding the international rules-based order and a free and open Indo-Pacific," adding that "we support Japan's decision to acquire new capabilities that strengthen regional deterrence, including counterstrike capabilities."

Japan's Minister of Defense Nobuo Kishi, younger brother of the late Prime Minister Shinzo Abe, declared last year that Japan's Self-Defense Forces (SDF) should have the right and capability to launch a "preemptive strike" against areas of some neighboring countries.

Salman Rafi Sheikh, a professor of politics at Lahore University in Pakistan, noted that the U.S. empire has instructed both of its two former World War II enemies, Germany and Japan, to rearm:

"Japan's drive to arm itself has an interesting parallel in Europe, where Germany, too, has decided to massively increase its total defense spending to 100 billion euros. With Washington actively supporting these critical changes to establish powerful militaries around its core rival states – Russia and China in Europe and Asia – new forms of conflict are likely to emerge, with prospects of major counter alliances on the horizon, too."

Salman Rafi Sheikh continues: "Japan's increasing defense budget comes on top of the full possibility of 'interoperability' between the U.S. and Japanese units, allowing the latter to 'practice its forward-deployed attack capabilities.' What is extremely important to note here is that the core purpose of the 'interoperability' is not defensive; it is offensive, which means that Japan's so-called 'pacifism' is nothing more than a rhetoric that Tokyo uses – and will continue to use – to mask its rapidly growing military preparedness against Russia and China.

"That this process is being actively supported by the U.S. is evident from Japanese Prime Minister Fumio Kishida's announcement, on the sidelines of Biden's Tokyo visit, to 'drastically strengthen' its military capabilities.

"According to a new economic policy draft released by the Kishida administration, the decision is a response to 'attempts to unilaterally change the status quo by forces in East Asia, making regional security increasingly severe.' If this assessment sounds vague, it is by design to camouflage Japan's rise as a new military power that can rival Russia and China as a U.S. ally.

"In fact, it is already acting as a U.S. ally against Russia in the Russia-Ukraine conflict. In April, Japanese officials announced that they will send defense equipment – drones and protective gear – to Ukraine to help the Ukrainian military fight the Russian forces.

"While Japan's Self-Defense Forces rules prohibit the transfer of defense products to other countries, Defence Minister Nobuo Kishi justified this transfer as 'commercial' and 'disused items.' More self-serving justifications will be invented to mask Japan's so-called 'pacifist militarization.'"

China's new 7 nm chip challenges U.S. sanctions aimed at strangling China's development.

Chris Fry | Nov. 6, 2023

The U.S. steps up its 'chip war' against socialist China

On October 17, Commerce Secretary Gina Raimondo announced new bans on the giant tech company Nvidia from sales of its advanced computer chips, particularly its advanced H800 and A800 products.

Raimondo claimed that this move was directed solely against the Chinese military. According to an October 18 CNN report, she said in August on her visit to China: "the administration was "laser-focused" on slowing the advancement of China's military. She emphasized that Washington had opted not to go further in restricting chips for other applications."

But on October 17, Raimondo made clear that the target of these sanctions against socialist China is much wider:

"The goal was to limit China's 'access to advanced semiconductors that could fuel breakthroughs in artificial intelligence and sophisticated computers'."

China's Foreign Ministry quickly responded:

"The US needs to stop politicizing and weaponizing trade and tech issues and stop destabilizing global industrial and supply chains," spokesperson Mao Ning told a press briefing. "We will closely follow the developments and firmly safeguard our rights and interests."

China has decided to cut off the U.S. from supplies of germanium and gallium, essential for manufacturing semiconductors.

Commerce secretary calls Huawei's computer chip breakthrough 'incredibly disturbing'

At a Senate hearing on October 5, Commerce Secretary Raimondo called the Chinese firm Huawei's new cellphone and its 7nm computer chip "incredibly disturbing." Why? It's because that chip was produced by the Chinese state-owned Semiconductor Manufacturing International Corporation (SMIC).

Both companies, Huawei and SMIC, have been "blacklisted" by both the Trump and Biden administrations to prevent them from developing advanced semiconductors and other computer technologies.

In 2018, Trump had gone so far as to have a top Huawei executive placed under house arrest in Canada for three years for supposedly violating U.S. sanctions against Iran.

The Biden administration has escalated its economic war with China, prohibiting not only U.S. companies from selling advanced computer technologies to Chinese companies but also other countries from doing so, such as South Korea, the Netherlands, and the computer companies based in Taiwan. U.S. "experts" had predicted that this move would take decades for China to overcome if it ever did.

An October 4 opinion piece in the New York Times details how the U.S. establishment uses international digital financial tools to bend their "junior partners" to their will over the sentiments of the populace in their own countries. The article discusses a recently published book: "Underground

Empire: How America Weaponized the Global Economy," by Henry Farrell of Johns Hopkins and Abraham Newman of Georgetown:

"These institutions include the dollar and the bank-messaging system known as Swift (the Society for Worldwide Interbank Financial Telecommunication), which is based in Belgium and run by an international board but vulnerable to American pressure. It helps that the rise of the internet has made the United States home to much of the wired world's circuitry and infrastructure, including, in our time, some of the major cloud computing centers of Amazon Web Services, Microsoft, and Google.

"The United States now has the ability to survey and influence the world's communications and supply chains, should it choose to. After the Sept. 11 [2001] attacks, it chose to. It bent the institutions to which it had access into a defensive (as it then saw things) weapon in the war on terror. 'To protect America,' Mr. Farrell and Mr. Newman write, 'Washington has slowly but surely turned thriving economic networks into tools of domination.'

"A study this past summer by the European Council on Foreign Relations found large majorities, 62 percent continent wide, would wish for Europe to remain neutral should the United States and China ever enter into conflict over Taiwan. Yet last April, when President Emmanuel Macron of France urged his fellow Europeans to preserve their 'strategic autonomy' in Sino-American matters and avoid getting swept up in 'a logic of bloc against bloc,' he was rebuffed, not just by American politicians but also by certain of his European allies."

Up until these imperialist sanctions, socialist China had obtained its semiconductor and other tech designs from a complex global network. Facing this U.S. blockade, the Chinese government began a robust campaign to develop its own semiconductor design capabilities. With this new Huawei success, it appears that socialist China has made a massive breakthrough.

Of course, in an example of extraordinary arrogance, the U.S. accused China's SMIC, a company that it had already sanctioned, of violating those sanctions by not asking the U.S. Commerce Department for "permission" to develop its own new computer chip and sell it to another Chinese company, Huawei.

Not only is the U.S. placing stricter requirements on computer chip sales by its own companies and its Western subordinates, but it has demanded that Taiwan rulers stop its companies from engaging with tech companies on the mainland.

An October 5 Benzinga article stated that a probe by the Bloomberg business website revealed that four companies based in Taiwan were helping to build semiconductor plants in the mainland. The linchpin of the entire U.S. strategy to counter China is Taiwan and the Trump/Biden threat to wage war to defend the island's "independence," breaking with the "One China" policy that the U.S. had agreed to in 1979.

Biden's much-touted anti-China "Chips and Science Act" program has hit a snag with the most important of Taiwan's tech companies – the Taiwan Semiconductor Manufacturing Company (TSMC). An August 28 article from the Guardian indicates that the company is eager to get the U.S. government money but is in no hurry to actually build the plant in Arizona or hire union workers:

- Eight months on, the Phoenix microchip plant – the centerpiece of Biden's $52.7bn US hi-tech manufacturing agenda – is struggling to get online.

- The plant's owner Taiwan Semiconductor Manufacturing Company (TSMC), the largest chip maker in the world, has pushed back plans to start manufacturing to 2025, blaming a lack of skilled labor. It is trying to fast-track visas for 500 Taiwanese workers. Unions, meanwhile, are accusing TSMC of inventing the skills shortage as an excuse to hire cheaper, foreign labor. Others point to safety issues at the plant.

A "presidential" election is slated in Taiwan in January 2024. Polls indicate that the pro-independence ruling party's candidate has only 33 percent popular support, while the three opposition candidates who oppose independence garner more than 50 percent support. They have yet to come up with a way to unify their opposition, but it still indicates that Taiwan's residents reject the Ukraine-style proxy war scenario that the Pentagon and the Biden White House are pushing.

Artificial Intelligence – the next front

Now, the U.S. is scrambling to prevent China from developing even more powerful semiconductors and other advanced technologies that would power Artificial Intelligence (AI) systems.

Of course, AI presents opportunities for greater profits in a capitalist society. Each worker becomes more "productive"; that is, she or he can produce more goods or services in less time. But since the value of each commodity or service is measured by the amount of "average" labor time to produce it, this same technical development drives down that value, forcing companies to "overproduce" to try to maintain their level of profits. This leads to the "bust" part of the capitalist cycle – recessions and depressions.

But this is not a problem in a socialist system, where production is socially owned and is driven by scientific planning, not profit. China has virtually eliminated poverty. President Johnson declared his "War on Poverty" in 1964, but just like his war against socialist Vietnam, poverty won and is still widespread here among the workers and oppressed communities.

And the capitalist class fears that artificial intelligence could be used under socialism to greatly enhance the coordination and accuracy of that scientific planning. The workers, through their Communist Party, could use it to far more capably direct their economy to meet the people's needs rather than fill the coffers of the banks and corporations.

The imperialist ruling class is keenly aware of the danger of this, not only in its economic competition with socialist China but also with the example of a powerful and prosperous socialist China lighting a revolutionary beacon to the global working class as to the possibilities with a new social system.

Source: Fighting Words

Gary Wilson | Dec. 21, 2023

Photo: U.S. Air Force

As recession looms: Spending soars for U.S. war operations

It's a war economy.

You may have heard of Bidenomics — Genocide Joe's economic policy. The New York Times reported last October that the White House was telling Democrats that Biden's reelection will be won because of Bidenomics. Since then, what's happened? Bidenomics has quietly disappeared from all Democratic campaign talk.

The National Priorities Project reports that Biden's military budget is one of the highest in history. "The Biden request calls for $886 billion in spending for the military and war preparations." The NPP points out that this is at the level of spending at the height of the Iraq and Afghanistan wars and is approaching the level of military spending during World War II.

In an October Oval Office Address, Biden said sending weapons to Ukraine is actually an investment in U.S. industry, strengthening the economy and creating new jobs. Politico quotes Biden: "As we replenish our stocks of weapons, we are partnering with the U.S. defense industry to increase our capacity … This supplemental request invests over $50 billion in the American defense industrial base … expanding production lines, strengthening the American economy and creating new American jobs."

So here's the thing. All the financial indicators point to a major recession soon. Is Biden attempting to divert an economic bust? Can a large-scale military buildup or even a war avoid a recession?

A war economy produces the means of destruction or subsistence for soldiers instead of profit-producing production and profit-producing workers. Bidenomics may keep unemployment levels from rising with low-wage, non-union jobs, but it's driving down the capitalist profit rate.

Financing the enormous military budget is the primary reason for the massive federal debt, and it led to the greatest bond market crash in history in October. You probably didn't hear about it. They don't like to talk about these things. The government issues bonds, called Treasuries, when they want to borrow money. That's how they've been paying for the massive military budget.

In the financial press, Bloomberg reported that Treasury bonds with maturities of 10 years or more plummeted 46%. That's just under the losses in the stock market when the dot-com bubble burst in 2000.

What's coming out of this is higher taxes and cuts in social spending to pay for the massive military buildup and warfare.

The current economic slowdown is because of general overproduction, with manufacturers facing excess inventory.

Economic growth (not slowdown) is the lifeblood of capitalism. Industrial production is not growing; it has stagnated for the past year.

On Dec. 4, Reuters reported that "makers of computer and electronic products said the 'economy appears to be slowing dramatically.' Miscellaneous manufacturing firms said, 'Customer orders have pushed into the first quarter of 2024, resulting in inflated end-of-year inventory. Producers of food, beverage, and tobacco reported that 'our executives have requested that we bring down inventory levels considerably.'"

Factories are now working at less than full capacity, but corporations are building more factories at a furious rate. On Dec. 2, there was a headline: "The Eyepopping Factory Construction Boom in the U.S."

Industrial capitalists are building new factories even as their current factories cannot run at their full capacity due to a lack of markets. As the new factories come online, the gap between the ability to produce and the market's ability to absorb the increasing volume of commodities at profitable prices is growing dramatically.

The growing gap between expanding production capacity and limited market demand is unsustainable. A recession looms.

Bidenomics a failure

As any worker will quickly confirm, Bidenomics is a failure. Really. Have prices rolled back? Overall, prices have surged by more than 17 percent since January 2021 — nearly 20 percent for food, more than 43 percent for gasoline, and 18 percent for housing, according to data from the U.S. Bureau of Labor Statistics.

Workers are fighting for and winning wage increases, but overall, for most workers, wages still lag behind inflation. 60% of the workforce is living paycheck to paycheck. Homelessness in the U.S. jumped to a record level in 2023, the highest number of people reported as experiencing homelessness since reporting began.

Anyway, as we've seen in our discussions today, the U.S. is engaged in war, hybrid war, economic war, and multiple kinds of warfare in several parts of the world. Genocide Joe's war on Gaza. The U.S.-NATO proxy war on Russia.

There is also the possibility of a U.S. and/or Israeli attack on Iran.

CBS News reported on a major deployment of U.S. warships to the region. The aircraft carrier USS Eisenhower's strike group arrived in the Red Sea in mid-November. An unknown number of nuclear submarines armed with hundreds of cruise missiles are there. The aircraft carrier USS Ford strike group is in the area in the Mediterranean along with at least five other battleship groups. CBS adds that 45,000 U.S. service members and contractors are now stationed in the Middle East.

U.S. Secretary of Defense Lloyd Austin just announced the start of Operation Prosperity Guardian, a naval operation in the Red Sea and Gulf of Aden targeting Yemen's Ansarallah-aligned armed forces and threatening Iran.

That's three fronts in U.S. imperialism's global war – Palestine, Russia, and Iran.

Of course, there's also the sanctions, economic warfare against Cuba, Venezuela, Zimbabwe, and others.

War buildup in Asia

Then, there are the war fronts against the Democratic People's Republic of Korea and China.

The U.S. has imposed sweeping sanctions on China's semiconductor industry, aiming to restrict China's advanced computing and supercomputing abilities and prevent it from becoming a global leader in semiconductors. The New York Times called the semiconductor blockade "an act of war." Saying, and I quote: "The controls essentially seek to eradicate, root and branch, China's entire ecosystem of advanced technology."

And then there is Taiwan.

Taiwan has been part of China for centuries. Japan colonized Taiwan in 1895 and Korea in 1910. After the victory of the Communist Party of China in 1949, the defeated Kuomintang took over Taiwan with U.S. support. The U.S. later acknowledged the People's Republic of China's sovereignty over Taiwan under the One China policy but never relinquished its de facto control.

Now, the U.S. has virtually dropped its One China policy and has started a massive military buildup in Taiwan combined with a significant naval buildup in the South China Sea.

Unlike previous administrations, including Donald Trump's, the Biden administration has not confirmed the One China policy. Responsible Statecraft reported that "Assistant Secretary of Defense for Indo-Pacific Security Affairs Ely Ratner made an unprecedented public statement by a serving senior U.S. official. In testimony before the Senate Committee on Foreign Relations, he stated that the island of Taiwan is strategically "critical to the region's security and critical to the defense of vital U.S. interests in the Indo-Pacific." He's saying that Taiwan is "ours."

In August, the U.S., Japan, and South Korea established what's being called an Asian NATO, a trilateral military cooperation agreement, including a joint missile defense system. This is aimed at both North Korea and China.

Biden's massive military budget must be paid for by the workers. The U.S. is imposing a wartime economy, hoping to rescue the capitalists from the coming economic collapse while at the same time threatening imperialist war around the globe.

Gary Wilson | Feb. 25, 2024

Unsustainable war machine: U.S. imperialism in crisis

General Smedley Butler said, "War is a racket." Wikipedia explains that he was referring to the war profiteers and the "imperialist motivations for U.S. foreign policy and wars."

A Guardian headline on Feb. 18 declared: "World's largest oil companies have made $281bn profit since invasion of Ukraine." Below the headline was the teaser: "Global Witness says the five 'super-majors' are the 'main winners of the war' while many struggle to heat their homes."

A Wall Street Journal headline on Feb. 18 declared: "How war in Europe boosts the U.S. economy."

The U.S./NATO proxy war in Ukraine against Russia "is good for the U.S. economy," the WSJ reports. "Industrial production in the U.S. defense and space sector has increased 17.5%."

The report continues, "Biden administration officials say that of the $60.7 billion earmarked for Ukraine in a $95 billion supplemental defense bill, 64% will actually flow back to the U.S. defense industrial base."

The WSJ adds that the $95 billion military aid package also includes funds earmarked for Israel and Taiwan.

That's war on three fronts.

The U.S. is in a steadily expanding military buildup of unprecedented proportions. But the economic basis for sustaining military expansion — for war on three fronts — is in virtual ruin.

After World War II, the United States was the world's leading imperialist economic and military force. As the predominant imperialist power, the U.S. had unrivaled political and military dominance over its imperialist rivals in Western Europe and Japan, as well as over developing countries and oppressed peoples globally.

In the early 1950s, the United States accounted for over 50% of global economic production. In 2023, the U.S. has fallen to about 26% of global gross domestic product (GDP), with China, Germany, and Japan all rising, according to the IMF. China's share of the global GDP surged from 2% in 1980 to 18% in 2021.

When adjusted for the cost of living (the IMF's PPP – purchasing power parity), the U.S. per capita GDP now ranks ninth in the world.

The basic industries of the U.S. have declined after decades of deindustrialization that began in the late 1970s.

In terms of capitalist production for profit, which involves competition for capitalist markets and the acquisition of sources of raw materials, the U.S. has become tremendously weakened as a world power. For instance, in its current heated military expansion, the U.S. has access to a fraction of the world's total production over what it had in the 1950s.

Consider the supply chain crisis during the COVID shutdown. COVID restrictions and lockdowns, especially in China, a major global manufacturing hub, led to shortages of components and products. Factories and ports in the U.S. stalled. Global supply chains are interconnected and interdependent, with many companies reliant on just-in-time inventory and single sources for parts.

While the economic base of U.S. imperialism has been contracting, the drive for military expansion has increased.

"U.S. military spending is at an all-time high," writes John Feffer at the Institute for Policy Studies. "From 2017 to 2023, the Pentagon's base budget increased by over 50%. For 2024, overall U.S. military spending — which includes the allotment for the Pentagon, the budget for nuclear weapons at the Department of Energy, and a few other items — will be $886 billion. With supplemental requests, like the current one for Ukraine and Israel, the total will approach $1 trillion, the highest military spending since World War II."

In October 2023, President Joe Biden said that the U.S. must be "the arsenal of democracy," echoing a 1940 call to arms by Franklin D. Roosevelt. Biden was emphasizing the wars in Ukraine and Gaza and the U.S. arms buildup in Taiwan.

The biggest part of the U.S. war buildup in the Pentagon budget is aimed at China.

The Modern War Institute at West Point says, "The U.S. military is attempting to quickly replenish diminished weapons stocks in its largest production ramp-up in decades. With an eye on its pacing threats and the risk of major conflict — with China, in particular — it is transitioning to modern platforms, including attack submarines, heavy bombers, and air defense systems, as well as new approaches to electric vehicles. Given its security assistance to Ukraine and recent military support to Israel, and conflict risks with China, it is simultaneously rearming with legacy munitions — 155-millimeter artillery, Javelin antitank missiles, and surface-to-air Stinger missiles."

Crises of a declining empire

So, the Pentagon has launched a military expansion of unprecedented proportions, while the economic basis for sustaining such an unbridled military buildup has been severely eroded.

The U.S. capitalist system is facing multiple crises.

The global production decline should not be confused with a capitalist overproduction crisis.

Crises of overproduction are usually called cyclical capitalist events or simply recessions in the media. Capitalism has had economic crises periodically since 1825. Capitalism goes through a boom and bust cycle every 10 years or so. Marx identified these cyclical events as crises of overproduction.

Capitalists produce goods and services only for profit and not for need. Production is disrupted when commodities can no longer be sold at a profit. Capitalist production can be effectively expanded, but the markets respond slowly, if at all. The overproduction is relative; that is, it's not that more is produced than is needed. It's that more is produced than can be sold at a profit.

A cyclical recession looms over the U.S. economy. Recessions are sweeping the capitalist countries. Japan, Britain, Ireland, and Finland are now in what Wall Street calls "technical recessions," which means at least two successive quarters of GDP contraction.

"This is only the tip of the iceberg," says one report. Denmark, Luxembourg, Moldova, and Estonia were already in recession. Six countries — Ecuador, Bahrain, Iceland, South Africa, Canada, and New Zealand — reported shrinking GDP in October. And six more — Malaysia, Thailand, Romania, Lithuania, Germany, and Colombia — reported GDP contraction in December.

Debt around $33 trillion

Heavy borrowing by the U.S. government has financed military expansion. The U.S. budget deficit doubled from 2022 to 2023. The overall debt now stands at around $33 trillion. That's the value of the combined economies of China, Japan, Germany, India and Britain.

Military spending is different than the capitalist market. Military spending goes to produce planes, tanks, missiles, and other defense systems.

These military products do not function like regular commodities. They do not compete with other commodities for buyers in the capitalist market. There is no concern about overproducing since they do not compete for buyers based on market demands.

Government loan-financed military spending raises industrial production but depresses the capitalist process of expansion. Capitalist production is not simply to meet consumer needs but to maximize surplus value (profits). A portion of the profits made are used to expand the means of production (machines, technology, infrastructure, etc.).

Military spending redirects production from expanded production of the means of production into producing the means of destruction. More capital is consumed than is created.

The very goal of capitalist production is not meeting consumer demand or social needs but maximizing extraction of surplus value or profit from workers. Expansion is a key means to keep profits growing. Without expansion, profits fall.

The total product of the military-industrial complex is devoid of usefulness. The vast sums borrowed for the military budget have flooded the world with dollars of decreasing value due to military spending for which there has been no material return.

"Military spending has been crowding out other spending," said Jason Furman, an economist at Harvard University. He noted that Vietnam War spending in the 1960s contributed to the soaring inflation at that time, which led to stagflation, the combination of high inflation and a slowing economy.

In the year 2000, the U.S. government debt was $3.5 trillion, equal to 35% of the GDP. By 2022, the debt was $24 trillion, equal to 95% of GDP. The single biggest source of this increase is military spending. According to the Watson Institute at Brown University, the cost of U.S. wars from fiscal year 2001 to fiscal year 2022 amounted to a whopping $8 trillion.

Forbes magazine recently noted that when adjusted for inflation, the U.S. bank leases and loans showed zero growth at the end of 2023. The capitalist economy simply cannot grow without sustained loan and lease growth. Zero growth means a contraction of the economy. "In simple terms, if this trend doesn't change, then we are most likely to see a recession," Forbes says.

On top of the periodic economic recessions inherent to capitalism, an even more severe crisis is plaguing U.S. monopoly capitalism. The decline of U.S. production and GDP and the rise of China, Germany, and Japan reveal the so-called competitive crisis: the loss of their competitive edge in the world market by significant elements of U.S. industry and finance.

The U.S. has slowly lost its dominant position in world trade and commerce.

Look at Boeing, a monopoly once dominant in the world aircraft industry in commercial and military production.

Barack Obama once quipped, "Other than — maybe — the CEO of Boeing, I don't know anyone who's done more to sell Boeing planes around the world than me."

Then-President Donald Trump said during a 2017 visit to a plant in South Carolina: "God bless you, may God bless the United States of America, and God bless Boeing." Boeing executive Patrick Shanahan was a Trump Secretary of Defense, the head of the Pentagon. Shanahan is also president and CEO of Spirit AeroSystems, which produced the defective parts for Boeing's 737 MAX airline.

Capitalist monopoly retards technological development, discourages inventiveness and innovation, and prevents the normal renewal, retooling, and reequipment of the basic industrial apparatus. If profits can be made by jacking up prices as a result of monopoly rather than by plant renewal, retooling, or modernization, then it becomes plain that the ruling class as a whole will opt for industrial production based on obsolete plant and equipment so long as profits can be maintained at a high level.

At Boeing, production was maximized for profit at the cost of air safety. In the 1970s, Boeing commanded 66% of the world market; now it is 41%.

A German-French-British consortium introduced the Airbus to compete with Boeing. Despite the occupying dominance of the U.S. and NATO, which has held Germany down by political and military means following the defeat of German imperialism in the Second World War, Airbus was mainly a German effort.

In 2019, Airbus displaced Boeing as the largest aerospace company by revenue due to the Boeing 737 MAX breakdowns.

German industrial engine stalls as U.S. guns and gas dictate terms

It's not an accident that Germany was the first casualty in the U.S./NATO proxy war on Russia.

In 2022, the European Union imported 40% of its gas from Russia. The primary route for gas from Russia was through the Nord Stream pipeline to Germany. Nord Stream 2 was built to at least double the capacity.

The U.S. opposed Nord Stream 2 since the pipeline's inception. Congressional efforts to block the pipeline imposed sanctions, with increasingly stringent sanctions legislation enacted in 2017, 2019, and 2020.

The Nord Stream 2 project was finished in September 2022 but was idle pending certification by Germany and the EU.

On Feb. 7, 2022, before any Russian military actions in Ukraine, President Joe Biden declared, "There will be no longer a Nord Stream 2. We will bring an end to it." (The U.S. Navy has since bombed and destroyed the pipeline.)

As the leading industrial economy in Europe, Germany had a heavy reliance on imported Russian oil, gas, and key minerals to fuel sectors like steel, chemicals, automotives, and complex machinery. This low-cost energy and raw material supply enabled the high productivity and exports behind Germany's economic preeminence.

Germany has been forced to replace low-priced Russian pipeline gas with high-priced U.S. liquified natural gas (LNG), making German industry less competitive.

Today, the U.S. is the top LNG exporter in the world and the biggest supplier of crude oil to Germany and the entire European Union at a much higher cost.

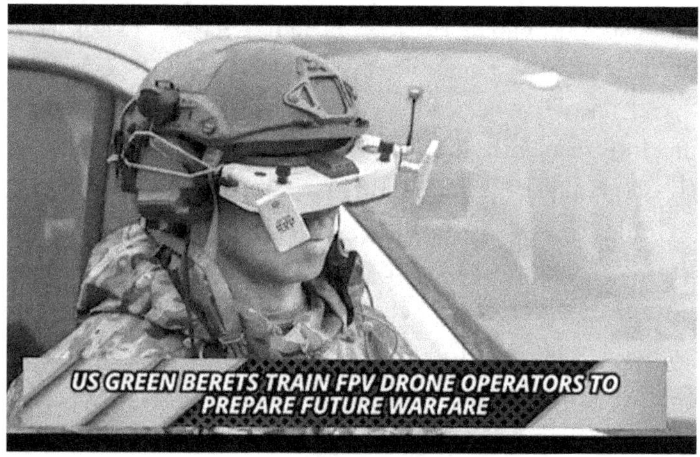
US GREEN BERETS TRAIN FPV DRONE OPERATORS TO
PREPARE FUTURE WARFARE

Screenshot

Gary Wilson | March 19, 2024

Washington's New Cold War: U.S. Special Forces train Taiwan troops in drone warfare

On March 14, Taiwan Defense Minister Chiu Kuo-cheng confirmed that U.S. Army Special Forces, specifically the "Green Berets," are permanently stationed in amphibious command centers in the Kinmen and Penghu islands.

The Green Berets are training Taiwanese forces on the use of military drones including the Black Hornet Nano, like those being used by U.S.-advised forces in Ukraine.

Previously, U.S. troops stationed in Taiwan were only temporary, not permanent. The permanent deployment of any U.S. troops to Taiwan breaches the "One China" policy.

China's sovereignty over Taiwan is internationally recognized. In 1972, in a joint communiqué, the U.S. acknowledged that "there is but one China and that Taiwan is a part of China."

While the U.S. officially recognizes that Taiwan is part of China, it has maintained a military presence on the island since the People's Liberation Army's victory in 1949, when the Chiang Kai-shek government fled to Taiwan. That presence was reduced in the 1970s after the adoption of the One China policy.

Now, as the BBC reported, "the U.S. is quietly arming Taiwan to the teeth."

"U.S. President Joe Biden recently signed off on a \$80m grant to Taiwan for the purchase of American military equipment. … The \$80m is not a loan," the BBC says. This is a departure from the earlier policy of only selling weapons to Taiwan.

The U.S. "is using its own money to send weapons to a place it officially doesn't recognize. This is happening under a program called Foreign Military Financing (FMF). …"

The FMF, under the State Department and separately funded through the Foreign Operations Appropriations Act, has been used to give some of the billions in military aid sent to Ukraine.

The BBC continues: "It has been used to send billions more to Afghanistan, Iraq, Israel and Egypt, and so on. But until now it has only ever been given to countries or organizations recognised by the United Nations. Taiwan is not. …

"After the U.S. switched diplomatic recognition from Taiwan to China in 1979, it continued to sell weapons to the island under the terms of the Taiwan Relations Act. … The U.S. State Department has been quick to deny [the FMF grant] implies any recognition of Taiwan."

The BBC quotes a top Taiwan politician who "says the \$80m is the tip of what could be a very large iceberg and notes that in July, President Biden used discretionary powers to approve the sale of military services and equipment worth \$500m to Taiwan." The report adds that Taiwan expects more than \$10 billion in military aid from the U.S.

The deployment of U.S. Army special forces near China's mainland, where they are establishing and conducting exercises with reconnaissance drones used for offensive military attacks, is an escalation in Washington's New Cold War against China.

Gary Wilson | March 15, 2024

Supporters of TikTok at the Capitol in Washington, as the House passed a bill that would lead to a nationwide ban of the popular video app. Photo Jamaal Bowman/bowman.house.gov

U.S. targets TikTok in escalating economic war against China

TikTok has emerged as a dominant force in social media, reshaping not just online culture but also extending its influence beyond the digital realm. Since its launch in 2016, TikTok has become one of the most popular social media platforms in the world, surpassing Facebook, Instagram, WhatsApp and YouTube in terms of downloads and engagement.

Through its unique format of short, audio-driven videos curated through algorithms, TikTok has propelled numerous artists, like Lil Nas X and Noah Kahan, into the mainstream spotlight. Music from Africa has gained a global audience. Even the Biden campaign is on TikTok with "BidenHQ," hoping to appeal to a younger audience than its base of retirees and Wall Street bankers.

Facebook is considered to be TikTok's biggest competitor.

"Meta clearly sees itself in a battle against TikTok for the hearts, minds, and attention spans of millennials, a significant chunk of the social media market. TikTok has experienced a staggering growth of users since the onset of the global pandemic, taking over a huge chunk of its competitor's audience," the Guardian reported.

So why do the Biden administration and Congress want to ban TikTok?

Are they all just fans of Mark Zuckerberg? Or in Zuckerberg's pocket? For sure, they've all probably had a few clubhouse dinners with Meta.

But this goes beyond Facebook. The target, and they clearly say this, is China. The ban passed by the House of Representatives is called the "Protecting Americans from Foreign Adversary Controlled Applications Act." China is the "foreign adversary."

A day after the House passed the bill, former U.S. Treasury Secretary Steven Mnuchin (under Donald Trump) announced he is putting together an investor group to take over TikTok. "This should be owned by U.S. businesses," he said.

TikTok's only "crime" is beating out Facebook and the others. They claim TikTok is somehow working with the Chinese military, but there isn't even a sliver of evidence of that.

Facebook has ties to the Pentagon (google "Fake Facebook and Instagram accounts promoting U.S. interests had ties to U.S. military" or "Big Tech Has Made Billions Off the

20-Year War on Terror"). Maybe we should ban Facebook. But that's another discussion.

Trump, Biden both target China

The U.S. government, under both the Trump and Biden administrations, has been escalating its economic war against China by imposing sanctions and restrictions on Chinese tech companies. The goal is to eradicate socialist China's entire system of advanced technology.

Reuters just reported on March 14 that while he was president, "Trump launched CIA covert influence operation against China." Reuters says that Trump had also given the CIA greater powers to launch offensive cyber operations against China and Russia. "Sources described the 2019 authorization uncovered by Reuters as a more ambitious operation."

The anti-TikTok propaganda is part of what Reuters calls a "covert messaging" operation.

"Covert propaganda campaigns were common during the Cold War," Reuters adds.

Some call it the New Cold War. However, the New Cold War cannot reproduce the old Cold War. China has emerged as a major manufacturing power, including in advanced technology, and is the largest trade partner for 70% of the world's countries. The U.S. no longer has the same dominant position in the global market.

The global landscape has changed dramatically since the Cold War era, but capitalism's fundamental contradictions persist today, mirroring those of the 1960s during the Vietnam War.

Financially and militarily, the U.S. empire is dangerously overextended.

Before the genocidal invasion of Gaza, the Biden administration was seeking to consolidate its dominance in the region by brokering Saudi Arabia's recognition of Israel. Now, the U.S. is spending billions of dollars on bombs and weapons systems for the Zionist regime's war on the Palestinian people.

For two years, the U.S. has engaged in the largest arms transfer in history, sending to Ukraine some $113.4 billion in "emergency funding" over and above the regular Pentagon budget. Growing war fatigue, however, has now reduced the funds.

The New York Times puts it this way:

"American support has sharply declined. House Republicans have blocked additional aid to Ukraine, and the Biden administration cannot send many more weapons. (The $300 million package announced this week will likely help Ukraine for only a few weeks.)"

In fact, the Times almost says, it is only U.S. weapons and ammunition that started this war and have kept it going. "It falls on the U.S. to supply Ukraine," the Times says. "The war is at a stalemate." The funds have run out.

U.S. imperialism considers socialist China's economic rise as its most significant contemporary challenge. It is resolute in thwarting Chinese industry from dominating the global markets. This ongoing "New Cold War" raises the specter of a potential war in the Pacific.

Stephen Millies | December 16, 2018

Trump is our enemy — not China

The lying bigot in the White House wants us to hate the People's Republic of China. Trump claims that China is ripping us off. How so?

In 2017, China exported $505 billion of goods to the United States, while the U.S. exported just $130 billion of stuff to China. If somebody gave you $505 in exchange for you paying just $130, who's ripping off whom?

China isn't the only country that runs a trade surplus with the U.S. The U.S. had a trillion-dollar trade deficit in 2017. Uncle Sam imported $2.4 trillion of goods while exporting $1.4 trillion (U.S. Census Bureau). Just 21% of those imports were from China.

In every year since 1975, the U.S. has imported more goods than it has exported, a result of deliberate deindustrialization.

Wall Street pulled the rug from much of U.S. manufacturing. Banksters and insurance companies found it much more profitable to speculate in real estate, particularly constructing luxury gentrified housing, and exploit workers first in low-wage Southern states, then other lower-wage countries.

It wasn't China that shut down nine of the ten GM plants in Flint, Mich. Or three Detroit factories in the mid-1980s, eliminating more than 10,000 jobs. Or the five North American factories that GM plans to "idle" in 2019, again throwing thousands of workers, their families, and communities into crisis and uncertainty. Why?

Now GM is chasing the dream of selling its cars to the 1.4 billion people in China, where wages and living conditions are rising. The capitalist system demands continual expansion. GM will build those cars in China, not Detroit, Texas, or Mexico.

U.S. finance capital smashed its dependence on Black labor in historically militant, urban centers like Detroit using plant closings and automation. In 1970, African Americans accounted for a quarter of U.S. autoworkers and steelworkers.

Vince Copeland described steel as "the most basic and crucial material in the construction of modern civilization." (Workers World, May 9, 1975) Copeland was a militant communist leader of steelworkers in Buffalo, N.Y.)

While the U.S. population increased from 212 million people in 1973 to 326 million in 2017, domestic steel production decreased in the same period from 151 million short tons to 90 million.

Even considering 34.6 million tons of steel imports — only 2 percent from the People's Republic of China — that's still a big drop in per capita domestic steel use. The result is a decaying infrastructure.

The only rail line west from New York City crosses the Hackensack River over Amtrak's 108-year-old Portal movable bridge. The bridge frequently gets stuck open, yet plans to replace it have been delayed for years.

'China has stood up'

China had endured over a century of colonial subjugation when, on Oct. 1, 1949, proclaiming the victorious revolution, Mao Zedong declared, "China has stood up," announcing the birth of the People's Republic of China.

In the 19th century, Britain actually launched the so-called Opium Wars against China to force the country to buy drugs. Right behind Britain were U.S. big-time opium merchants like Warren Delano, a grandfather of President Franklin Delano Roosevelt.

The Chinese Revolution ended this humiliation. Universal literacy has been achieved, including for people belonging to minority nationalities reading their own languages.

China graduates 1.3 million engineers a year, a million more than the U.S. figure (Boston Globe, May 22, 2017). While the Portal bridge in the U.S. gets regularly stuck open, China has built more miles of high-speed rail than the rest of the world combined.

The Chinese Revolution was a tremendous victory against racism.

According to Pentagon Papers whistleblower Daniel Ellsberg, the Pentagon had plans in the early 1960s to kill 300 million Chinese people in a nuclear war. (TheRealNews.

com, Nov. 9) Earlier, during the U.S. invasion of Korea, tens of thousands of Chinese volunteers — including Mao Anying, Mao Zedong's eldest son — died fighting alongside their Korean comrades to defeat U.S. Gen. Douglas MacArthur.

So why did the U.S. ruling class agree to trade with China?

It was a case of divide and conquer. U.S. markets were opened to China with the aim of splitting the socialist camp, which in the 1970s extended from Berlin in Europe to Ho Chi Minh City in Asia, as well as Cuba, Southern Yemen, Ethiopia, and other African countries.

Wall Street wasn't seeking to help China but rather to defeat the Soviet Union. The USSR's overthrow was a tragedy, just like the overthrow of the Reconstruction governments in the U.S. South, which empowered the Ku Klux Klan.

When all is said and done, the Pentagon has never given up on defeating China. Hundreds of U.S. nuclear missiles are aimed at it. The U.S. continues to keep Taiwan province from reuniting with the People's Republic.

Friendship not hate

Putting tariffs on imports will not bring any factories back. The resulting higher prices will be a wage cut for millions of workers.

Automation alone has destroyed millions of union jobs in the U.S. Capitalist decay and union busting have done the rest.

China bashing is poison and will inevitably lead to racist attacks on Asian Americans. The Chinese American Vincent Chin was beaten to death in Detroit on June 23, 1982, because of Japan bashing by the capitalist-owned media.

Like the African American Sean Bell, whom the cops fired 50 shots at, Vincent Chin was killed on what was supposed to be his wedding day.

In his autobiography, Malcolm X describes how much the Chinese Revolution inspired him while he was in jail. Mao Zedong welcomed the Black revolutionaries Mabel and Robert Williams to China, who had led armed self-defense against the Klan in Monroe, N.C.

The Haymarket Martyrs — George Engel, Adolph Fischer, Albert Parsons, and August Spies — were hanged in Chicago's Cook County Jail on Nov. 11, 1887, because they fought for the eight-hour workday. Exactly 56 years earlier, Nat Turner, the leader of a great insurrection of enslaved Africans, was hanged in Virginia.

It was only through the international cooperation of workers that the eight-hour workday was won in many countries. British workers stopped English landlords and capitalists from militarily intervening on the side of the slave masters' confederacy during the U.S. Civil War.

We need the same type of solidarity today. The U.S. labor movement needs to establish ties with the 300 million-member All-China Federation of Trade Unions, not unite with GM and other corporations and banks whose sole objective is expanding their control over the world and profits.

China bashing will not stop a single eviction, foreclosure, or utility cutoff in U.S. neighborhoods. Attacking China will not stop any more killings by police or free any of the 2.2 million poor people in jail.

Our enemy is in the corporate boardrooms, not China.

Index

WAR & LENIN
in the 21st Century

NEW - Updated to include U.S. complicity in the Gaza genocide and military profiteering.

Included in Gary Wilson's book is VI Lenin's pamphlet:
'Imperialism, the Highest Stage of Capitalism'

Vladimir Lenin, the revolutionary leader of the Soviet Union and a key contributor to Marxist theory, wrote **"Imperialism, the Highest Stage of Capitalism"** in 1916, more than a century ago. It remains an influential critique of imperialism.

When WWI broke out, Lenin's main interest was promoting a socialist revolution to end the war. He exposed the war's economic roots and identified imperialism's key features: monopoly capitalism, finance capital, the export of capital, and colonialism – the imperialist division of the world.

Does Lenin's analysis of imperialism hold up today?

The U.S. emerged from WWII as the world's most powerful imperialist country, it established the U.S. dollar as the international currency and engages in endless wars. As in Lenin's time, the conclusion is that socialist revolution will end imperialist war, enabling workers to meet their own needs.

Available in paperback or kindle at tinyurl.com/LeninAndWar